Stellar Seeds

Stellar Seeds

Matthew Petchinsky

publisher logo

CONTENTS

Stellar Seeds: The Cosmic Guide to Growing with Astrology
By: Matthew Petchinsky

Introduction: Astrology and Gardening - An Ancient Connection

Introduction to the Concept of Combining Astrology with Gardening

For centuries, humans have looked to the stars for guidance, drawing connections between celestial movements and earthly events. Astrology, the study of the influence of celestial bodies on human affairs, has a rich history intertwined with various aspects of life, including agriculture. Gardening, an essential practice for sustenance and beauty, has long been influenced by astrological principles. By aligning gardening activities with the rhythms of the cosmos, we can enhance plant growth, improve yields, and create more harmonious gardens.

Astrology offers a unique lens through which we can understand the natural world and our place within it. It provides a framework for interpreting the influence of the Sun, Moon, planets, and stars on our environment. When we combine astrology with gardening, we are tapping into a time-honored tradition that recognizes the interconnectedness of all life and the profound impact of celestial cycles on plant growth and development.

Historical Context

The connection between astrology and gardening dates back to ancient civilizations. The Babylonians, Egyptians, and Greeks all practiced forms of astrology that included agricultural considerations. They observed the sky and noted the positions of celestial bodies to determine the best times for planting, harvesting, and other agricultural activities.

Ancient Babylon

The Babylonians, one of the earliest civilizations to develop an astrological system, used their knowledge of the stars to guide their agricultural practices. They created detailed calendars that included information on lunar phases and planetary positions, which were crucial for determining the optimal times for sowing and reaping crops.

Ancient Egypt

In Ancient Egypt, the heliacal rising of the star Sirius signaled the annual flooding of the Nile, an event that was vital for agriculture. Egyptian farmers relied on this celestial event to plan their planting and harvesting schedules. The Egyptians also developed a zodiac system, incorporating it into their agricultural practices to enhance crop yields.

Ancient Greece and Rome

The Greeks and Romans further refined the practice of agricultural astrology. The Greek philosopher Theophrastus wrote extensively about the influence of celestial bodies on plants, while the Roman poet Virgil included astrological references in his agricultural writings. The Romans developed the "Agricultural Calendar," which detailed the best times for planting and harvesting based on the positions of the stars and planets.

The Benefits of Aligning Planting and Plant Care with Celestial Cycles

Modern gardening can greatly benefit from the wisdom of ancient astrological practices. By aligning planting and plant care with celestial cycles, we can harness the natural rhythms of the cosmos to create more productive and harmonious gardens. Here are some key benefits of integrating astrology into gardening:

Enhanced Plant Growth

Astrological gardening takes into account the influence of the Moon, Sun, and planets on plant growth. The Moon, for instance, has a significant impact on water movement within plants. Planting during specific lunar phases can enhance seed germination, root development, and overall plant vitality. For example, the waxing Moon is an ideal time for planting above-ground crops, while the waning Moon is better suited for root crops.

Improved Soil Health

Celestial cycles also affect soil health. By timing soil preparation and fertilization according to astrological principles, gardeners can improve soil fertility and structure. For instance, the Full Moon is a powerful time for enriching the soil with compost and organic matter, as the lunar energy aids in the decomposition and nutrient assimilation processes.

Pest and Disease Management

Astrological gardening can help manage pests and diseases more effectively. Certain celestial events, such as planetary alignments and lunar phases, can influence pest behavior and plant susceptibility to diseases. By aligning planting and maintenance activities with these cycles, gardeners can reduce pest infestations and promote plant resilience.

Harmonious Gardens

Gardening in harmony with celestial cycles creates a more balanced and harmonious environment. Astrological gardening acknowledges the interconnectedness of all living things and fosters a deeper connection between the gardener and the natural world. This holistic approach encourages mindfulness and a greater appreciation for the rhythms of nature.

Timing and Planning

Astrology provides a valuable tool for timing and planning gardening activities. Detailed astrological calendars can guide gardeners on the best times for planting, pruning, harvesting, and other essential tasks. This strategic approach maximizes the effectiveness of gardening efforts and ensures that plants receive optimal care throughout their growth cycles.

Conclusion

Combining astrology with gardening is not just a revival of ancient practices; it is a recognition of the timeless wisdom that the cosmos offers. By understanding and applying astrological principles to gardening, we can create more vibrant, healthy, and productive gardens. This introduction has provided a glimpse into the rich history and numerous benefits of astrological gardening. As you delve deeper into the chapters of this book, you will discover practical techniques and insights that will help you align your gardening practices with the celestial rhythms, fostering a deeper connection with nature and enhancing your gardening success.

Embrace the ancient connection between astrology and gardening, and let the stars guide your green thumb to new heights of harmony and productivity.

Part 1: The Zodiac Signs and Gardening

Chapter 1: Aries: The Fiery Initiator
Characteristics of Aries

Aries, the first sign of the zodiac, is ruled by Mars, the planet of action and energy. Known as the "Fiery Initiator," Aries is associated with boldness, enthusiasm, and a pioneering spirit. This cardinal fire sign embodies the qualities of leadership, courage, and dynamism. Aries individuals are often seen as trailblazers who are unafraid to take risks and embark on new ventures. In the context of gardening, the Aries influence encourages a proactive and energetic approach to planting and nurturing a garden.

Key Traits of Aries:

- **Element:** Fire
- **Ruling Planet:** Mars
- **Symbol:** The Ram
- **Modality:** Cardinal
- **Attributes:** Bold, energetic, assertive, pioneering, courageous, impulsive

Suitable Plants for Aries

Given Aries' dynamic and vigorous nature, the best plants for an Aries-influenced garden are those that thrive under intense conditions and display vibrant, fiery characteristics. These plants should be hardy, fast-growing, and often brightly colored, reflecting the bold spirit of Aries.

Ideal Plants for Aries:

1. **Peppers:**
   - **Varieties:** Bell peppers, chili peppers, habaneros
   - **Characteristics:** Bright colors, heat-tolerant, rapid growth
   - **Benefits:** High in vitamins, adds spice to meals

2. **Radishes:**
     - **Varieties:** Cherry Belle, French Breakfast, Watermelon radish
     - **Characteristics:** Fast-growing, hardy, vibrant colors
     - **Benefits:** Rich in antioxidants, quick harvest time
3. **Tomatoes:**
     - **Varieties:** Beefsteak, Cherry, Roma
     - **Characteristics:** Vigorous growth, requires strong support, high yield
     - **Benefits:** Nutrient-rich, versatile in cooking
4. **Marigolds:**
     - **Varieties:** African, French, Signet
     - **Characteristics:** Bright orange and yellow flowers, pest-resistant
     - **Benefits:** Natural pest deterrent, attracts beneficial insects
5. **Basil:**
     - **Varieties:** Sweet Basil, Thai Basil, Purple Basil
     - **Characteristics:** Fast-growing, aromatic, heat-tolerant
     - **Benefits:** Enhances flavor in culinary dishes, medicinal properties

Best Gardening Practices for Aries

Aries gardeners are known for their enthusiasm and readiness to dive into new projects. However, their impulsive nature means they might benefit from a structured approach to ensure sustained success in their gardening endeavors. Here are some best practices tailored to Aries' characteristics:

Planning and Preparation

- **Start Early:** Utilize Aries' proactive nature by planning the garden layout and gathering materials before the planting season begins.

- **Prepare the Soil:** Aries' energy is well-suited for intensive tasks. Take the time to enrich the soil with compost and organic matter to ensure a fertile base for plant growth.

Planting

- **Direct Sowing:** Aries' impatience for results makes direct sowing of seeds, such as radishes and marigolds, an ideal choice for quick germination and growth.
- **Transplanting:** For plants like tomatoes and peppers, start seeds indoors and transplant seedlings into the garden once they are strong enough. Aries gardeners can enjoy the process of nurturing young plants.

Maintenance

- **Regular Watering:** Ensure consistent watering, especially during dry spells. Aries' enthusiasm can sometimes lead to over-watering, so aim for balanced moisture levels.
- **Pruning and Training:** Use Aries' assertiveness to regularly prune and train plants like tomatoes, encouraging healthy growth and higher yields.

Pest and Weed Control

- **Active Monitoring:** Aries' vigilance is beneficial for monitoring and addressing pest and weed issues promptly. Use natural pest deterrents like marigolds and basil to keep harmful insects at bay.
- **Hand Weeding:** Channel Aries' energetic nature into regular hand weeding to maintain a tidy and healthy garden.

Optimal Planting Times for Aries

Timing is crucial for successful gardening. Aligning planting activities with astrological influences can enhance plant growth and overall garden vitality. Here are the optimal planting times for Aries-associated plants:

Peppers

- **Optimal Time:** Early spring, when the soil has warmed
- **Lunar Phase:** Waxing Moon (for above-ground crops)

Radishes

- **Optimal Time:** Early spring and late summer
- **Lunar Phase:** New Moon (for quick germination and growth)

Tomatoes

- **Optimal Time:** Late spring, after the last frost
- **Lunar Phase:** First Quarter Moon (to promote vigorous growth)

Marigolds

- **Optimal Time:** Spring, after the last frost
- **Lunar Phase:** Waxing Gibbous (for strong flowering)

Basil

- **Optimal Time:** Late spring to early summer
- **Lunar Phase:** Waxing Crescent (to encourage lush foliage)

Conclusion

Embracing the fiery energy of Aries in your garden can lead to a vibrant and productive growing season. By selecting suitable plants like peppers, radishes, tomatoes, marigolds, and basil, and following tailored gardening practices, you can harness the pioneering spirit of Aries to create a dynamic and flourishing garden. Aligning planting times with celestial cycles further enhances the connection between the cosmos and your garden, ensuring that your efforts are rewarded with abundant growth and bountiful harvests.

Aries gardeners, with their bold and energetic approach, are well-equipped to lead the way in astrological gardening, setting the stage for a successful and satisfying gardening experience.

Chapter 2: Taurus: The Earthy Sustainer

Characteristics of Taurus

Taurus, the second sign of the zodiac, is ruled by Venus, the planet of love, beauty, and fertility. Known as the "Earthy Sustainer," Taurus embodies stability, patience, and a deep connection to the physical world. This fixed earth sign is associated with perseverance, practicality, and a love for nature and all things beautiful. Taurus individuals are often seen as reliable, hardworking, and dedicated, making them excellent gardeners who appreciate the process of nurturing and sustaining plant life.

Key Traits of Taurus:

- **Element:** Earth
- **Ruling Planet:** Venus
- **Symbol:** The Bull
- **Modality:** Fixed
- **Attributes:** Patient, reliable, practical, persistent, sensual

Suitable Plants for Taurus

Given Taurus' affinity for the earth and beauty, the best plants for a Taurus-influenced garden are those that are robust, grounded, and aesthetically pleasing. These plants should thrive under stable conditions and reward the gardener with beautiful blooms or nutritious yields.

Ideal Plants for Taurus:

1. **Root Vegetables:**
   - **Varieties:** Carrots, beets, potatoes, turnips
   - **Characteristics:** Hardy, nutrient-rich, deeply connected to the earth
   - **Benefits:** High in vitamins and minerals, long storage life
2. **Roses:**
   - **Varieties:** Hybrid tea roses, floribunda, climbing roses

- **Characteristics:** Beautiful blooms, fragrant, requires care and attention
- **Benefits:** Adds beauty and fragrance to the garden, symbol of love and beauty

3. **Lavender:**
    - **Varieties:** English lavender, French lavender, Spanish lavender
    - **Characteristics:** Hardy, aromatic, drought-tolerant
    - **Benefits:** Calming fragrance, medicinal properties, attracts pollinators

4. **Thyme:**
    - **Varieties:** Common thyme, lemon thyme, creeping thyme
    - **Characteristics:** Hardy, aromatic, low-maintenance
    - **Benefits:** Culinary herb, medicinal uses, ground cover

5. **Blueberries:**
    - **Varieties:** Highbush, lowbush, rabbiteye
    - **Characteristics:** Hardy, perennial, nutrient-rich
    - **Benefits:** High in antioxidants, long harvest season

Best Gardening Practices for Taurus

Taurus gardeners are known for their patience and dedication, making them well-suited for nurturing plants that require consistent care and attention. Their practical approach ensures that their gardens are well-maintained and productive. Here are some best practices tailored to Taurus' characteristics:

Planning and Preparation

- **Prepare Thoroughly:** Taurus' methodical nature benefits from detailed planning and preparation. Ensure the soil is well-prepared and enriched with compost and organic matter before planting.

- **Mulching:** Use mulch to retain moisture, suppress weeds, and improve soil health. Taurus gardeners appreciate the long-term benefits of mulching.

Planting

- **Direct Sowing:** Root vegetables like carrots and beets can be sown directly into the soil. Ensure the soil is loose and well-drained for optimal root development.
- **Transplanting:** For plants like roses and blueberries, start with healthy seedlings or cuttings. Taurus' patience is ideal for carefully transplanting and establishing these plants.

Maintenance

- **Consistent Watering:** Taurus' reliability ensures regular watering, essential for plants like roses and blueberries. Water deeply to encourage strong root growth.
- **Pruning and Deadheading:** Regularly prune and deadhead roses to promote healthy growth and prolonged blooming. Taurus' attention to detail is perfect for this task.

Pest and Weed Control

- **Natural Remedies:** Use natural pest deterrents like neem oil or companion planting to protect plants from pests. Taurus gardeners value sustainable practices.
- **Regular Weeding:** Maintain a weed-free garden by regularly hand-weeding and using mulch to suppress weed growth.

Optimal Planting Times for Taurus

Timing is crucial for successful gardening. Aligning planting activities with astrological influences can enhance plant growth and overall garden vitality. Here are the optimal planting times for Taurus-associated plants:

Root Vegetables

- **Optimal Time:** Early spring and late summer
- **Lunar Phase:** New Moon (for quick germination and growth)

Roses

- **Optimal Time:** Spring or fall, depending on the climate
- **Lunar Phase:** Waxing Moon (to encourage strong root establishment)

Lavender

- **Optimal Time:** Late spring to early summer
- **Lunar Phase:** First Quarter Moon (for vigorous growth)

Thyme

- **Optimal Time:** Spring
- **Lunar Phase:** Waxing Crescent (to promote lush foliage)

Blueberries

- **Optimal Time:** Spring
- **Lunar Phase:** Waxing Gibbous (for strong flowering and fruiting)

Conclusion

Embracing the earthy energy of Taurus in your garden can lead to a stable and productive growing season. By selecting suitable plants like root vegetables, roses, lavender, thyme, and blueberries, and following tailored gardening practices, you can harness the sustaining spirit of Taurus to create a beautiful and bountiful garden. Aligning planting times with celestial cycles further enhances the connection between the cosmos and your garden, ensuring that your efforts are rewarded with abundant growth and successful harvests.

Taurus gardeners, with their patience and dedication, are well-equipped to nurture and sustain a flourishing garden, setting the stage for a harmonious and fulfilling gardening experience. By working in harmony with the rhythms of nature, Taurus can create a garden that not only thrives but also reflects the beauty and stability of the Earth.

Chapter 3: Gemini: The Airy Communicator
Characteristics of Gemini

Gemini, the third sign of the zodiac, is ruled by Mercury, the planet of communication and intellect. Known as the "Airy Communicator," Gemini embodies curiosity, adaptability, and a lively spirit. This mutable air sign is associated with duality, versatility, and a constant quest for knowledge and new experiences. Gemini individuals are often seen as social butterflies who thrive on variety and mental stimulation. In the context of gardening, the Gemini influence encourages a dynamic and versatile approach to planting and nurturing a garden.

Key Traits of Gemini:

- **Element:** Air
- **Ruling Planet:** Mercury
- **Symbol:** The Twins
- **Modality:** Mutable
- **Attributes:** Curious, adaptable, communicative, versatile, energetic

Suitable Plants for Gemini

Given Gemini's dynamic and versatile nature, the best plants for a Gemini-influenced garden are those that grow quickly, adapt well to different conditions, and often exhibit a lively, airy quality. These plants should thrive under varying conditions and reward the gardener with both aesthetic beauty and practical uses.

Ideal Plants for Gemini:

1. **Herbs:**
    - **Varieties:** Basil, mint, parsley, cilantro, thyme
    - **Characteristics:** Fast-growing, aromatic, versatile

- ◦ **Benefits:** Culinary and medicinal uses, attracts pollinators, easy to grow

2. **Climbers and Vines:**
   - ◦ **Varieties:** Morning glories, clematis, ivy, wisteria
   - ◦ **Characteristics:** Rapid growth, adaptable, decorative
   - ◦ **Benefits:** Adds vertical interest, provides shade and privacy, attracts pollinators

3. **Lettuce:**
   - ◦ **Varieties:** Romaine, butterhead, leaf lettuce, iceberg
   - ◦ **Characteristics:** Quick-growing, various textures and colors, adaptable
   - ◦ **Benefits:** Nutrient-rich, multiple harvests per season

4. **Snapdragons:**
   - ◦ **Varieties:** Rocket, butterfly, dwarf
   - ◦ **Characteristics:** Brightly colored flowers, adaptable, easy to grow
   - ◦ **Benefits:** Long blooming period, attracts pollinators, ornamental

5. **Peas:**
   - ◦ **Varieties:** Sugar snap peas, garden peas, snow peas
   - ◦ **Characteristics:** Climbing habit, quick-growing, nitrogen-fixing
   - ◦ **Benefits:** Nutrient-rich, improves soil fertility, multiple harvests

Best Gardening Practices for Gemini

Gemini gardeners are known for their curiosity and adaptability, making them well-suited for experimenting with various plants and gardening techniques. Their versatile approach ensures that their gardens are dynamic and ever-evolving. Here are some best practices tailored to Gemini's characteristics:

Planning and Preparation

- **Diversify Planting:** Gemini's love for variety benefits from a diverse garden plan. Include a mix of herbs, climbers, vegetables, and flowers to keep the garden interesting and dynamic.
- **Raised Beds and Containers:** Utilize raised beds and containers to allow flexibility in planting locations and easier management of different plant types.

Planting

- **Succession Planting:** Take advantage of Gemini's energetic nature by practicing succession planting. This involves planting crops in intervals to ensure continuous harvests throughout the growing season.
- **Companion Planting:** Gemini's communicative traits make companion planting ideal. Pairing compatible plants, such as herbs with vegetables, can enhance growth and deter pests.

Maintenance

- **Frequent Monitoring:** Gemini's curiosity drives frequent garden inspections. Regularly check for pests, diseases, and growth progress to address issues promptly.
- **Pruning and Training:** Use Gemini's adaptability to train climbers and vines on trellises or supports. Regular pruning will promote healthy growth and maintain plant shape.

Pest and Weed Control

- **Natural Solutions:** Embrace Gemini's versatility by using natural pest control methods, such as introducing beneficial insects and using organic sprays.

- **Mulching:** Apply mulch to suppress weeds, retain moisture, and improve soil health. Gemini gardeners can experiment with different types of mulch to find the best fit.

Optimal Planting Times for Gemini

Timing is crucial for successful gardening. Aligning planting activities with astrological influences can enhance plant growth and overall garden vitality. Here are the optimal planting times for Gemini-associated plants:

Herbs

- **Optimal Time:** Spring and early summer
- **Lunar Phase:** Waxing Crescent (to promote lush foliage)

Climbers and Vines

- **Optimal Time:** Spring
- **Lunar Phase:** Waxing Gibbous (for strong growth and flowering)

Lettuce

- **Optimal Time:** Early spring and fall
- **Lunar Phase:** New Moon (for quick germination and growth)

Snapdragons

- **Optimal Time:** Spring and fall
- **Lunar Phase:** First Quarter Moon (to encourage vigorous blooming)

Peas

- **Optimal Time:** Early spring and late summer
- **Lunar Phase:** Waxing Crescent (for robust growth and productivity)

Conclusion

Embracing the airy and communicative energy of Gemini in your garden can lead to a lively and versatile growing season. By selecting suitable plants like herbs, climbers, lettuce, snapdragons, and peas, and following tailored gardening practices, you can harness the dynamic spirit of Gemini to create a vibrant and ever-changing garden. Aligning planting times with celestial cycles further enhances the connection between the cosmos and your garden, ensuring that your efforts are rewarded with abundant growth and continuous harvests.

Gemini gardeners, with their curiosity and adaptability, are well-equipped to experiment with various plants and techniques, setting the stage for an engaging and innovative gardening experience. By working in harmony with the rhythms of nature, Gemini can create a garden that not only thrives but also reflects the lively and versatile qualities of the Airy Communicator.

Chapter 4: Cancer: The Watery Nurturer
Characteristics of Cancer

Cancer, the fourth sign of the zodiac, is ruled by the Moon, which governs emotions, intuition, and nurturing qualities. Known as the "Watery Nurturer," Cancer embodies sensitivity, empathy, and a deep connection to home and family. This cardinal water sign is associated with protection, care, and an instinctual drive to nurture and sustain life. Cancer individuals are often seen as compassionate and supportive, making them excellent gardeners who excel in creating a nurturing environment for plants to thrive.

Key Traits of Cancer:

- **Element:** Water
- **Ruling Planet:** Moon
- **Symbol:** The Crab
- **Modality:** Cardinal
- **Attributes:** Nurturing, intuitive, protective, empathetic, home-loving

Suitable Plants for Cancer

Given Cancer's nurturing and intuitive nature, the best plants for a Cancer-influenced garden are those that require care and attention, thrive in moist conditions, and often have a soothing or calming presence. These plants should resonate with Cancer's love for home and family, providing both beauty and sustenance.

Ideal Plants for Cancer:

1. **Leafy Greens:**
   - **Varieties:** Lettuce, spinach, kale, Swiss chard
   - **Characteristics:** Quick-growing, nutrient-rich, thrives in cool, moist conditions

- **Benefits:** High in vitamins and minerals, multiple harvests per season

2. **Moonflowers:**
   - **Varieties:** Ipomoea alba
   - **Characteristics:** Night-blooming, fragrant, large white flowers
   - **Benefits:** Adds beauty and fragrance to night gardens, attracts nocturnal pollinators

3. **Water Lilies:**
   - **Varieties:** Hardy water lilies, tropical water lilies
   - **Characteristics:** Floating leaves, colorful blooms, thrives in ponds and water gardens
   - **Benefits:** Enhances water features, provides habitat for aquatic life

4. **Ferns:**
   - **Varieties:** Boston fern, maidenhair fern, staghorn fern
   - **Characteristics:** Lush green foliage, prefers shade and moisture
   - **Benefits:** Adds greenery to shady areas, improves air quality

5. **Camellias:**
   - **Varieties:** Camellia japonica, Camellia sasanqua
   - **Characteristics:** Evergreen shrubs, large, colorful blooms, prefers acidic soil
   - **Benefits:** Adds year-round beauty, provides early spring and winter flowers

Best Gardening Practices for Cancer

Cancer gardeners are known for their nurturing and protective nature, making them well-suited for creating a garden that feels like a sanctuary. Their intuitive approach ensures that their plants receive the care and attention they need to thrive. Here are some best practices tailored to Cancer's characteristics:

Planning and Preparation

- **Create a Sanctuary:** Cancer's love for home and family benefits from creating a garden that feels like a peaceful retreat. Include seating areas, water features, and pathways to enhance the garden's sanctuary-like quality.
- **Soil Enrichment:** Use Cancer's nurturing nature to enrich the soil with compost, organic matter, and mulches to create a fertile environment for plant growth.

Planting

- **Moisture-Retaining Techniques:** Cancer's affinity for water makes moisture-retaining techniques essential. Use mulches, drip irrigation, and moisture-retentive soil to keep plants hydrated.
- **Shade Gardening:** For plants like ferns and camellias, create shaded areas using shade cloths or plant them under trees to protect them from harsh sunlight.

Maintenance

- **Consistent Watering:** Cancer's protective nature ensures regular and deep watering, especially for plants that thrive in moist conditions. Avoid over-watering by monitoring soil moisture levels.
- **Pruning and Deadheading:** Use Cancer's attention to detail to regularly prune and deadhead plants like camellias and leafy greens to promote healthy growth and prolonged blooming.

Pest and Weed Control

- **Natural Remedies:** Embrace Cancer's intuitive approach by using natural pest control methods, such as introducing beneficial insects and using organic sprays. Companion planting can also deter pests naturally.

- **Hand Weeding:** Maintain a weed-free garden by regularly hand-weeding and using mulch to suppress weed growth. Cancer gardeners enjoy the hands-on care of their garden.

Optimal Planting Times for Cancer

Timing is crucial for successful gardening. Aligning planting activities with astrological influences can enhance plant growth and overall garden vitality. Here are the optimal planting times for Cancer-associated plants:

Leafy Greens

- **Optimal Time:** Early spring and fall
- **Lunar Phase:** New Moon (for quick germination and growth)

Moonflowers

- **Optimal Time:** Late spring to early summer
- **Lunar Phase:** Waxing Crescent (to encourage strong flowering)

Water Lilies

- **Optimal Time:** Spring and early summer
- **Lunar Phase:** First Quarter Moon (to promote vigorous growth)

Ferns

- **Optimal Time:** Spring
- **Lunar Phase:** Waxing Crescent (to encourage lush foliage)

Camellias

- **Optimal Time:** Late fall to early spring (depending on the climate)
- **Lunar Phase:** Waxing Gibbous (for strong root establishment)

Conclusion

Embracing the watery and nurturing energy of Cancer in your garden can lead to a serene and flourishing growing season. By selecting suitable plants like leafy greens, moonflowers, water lilies, ferns, and camellias, and following tailored gardening practices, you can harness the caring spirit of Cancer to create a beautiful and nurturing garden. Aligning planting times with celestial cycles further enhances the connection between the cosmos and your garden, ensuring that your efforts are rewarded with abundant growth and successful harvests.

Cancer gardeners, with their nurturing and intuitive approach, are well-equipped to create a garden that feels like a sanctuary, setting the stage for a peaceful and fulfilling gardening experience. By working in harmony with the rhythms of nature, Cancer can create a garden that not only thrives but also reflects the soothing and protective qualities of the Watery Nurturer.

Chapter 5: Leo: The Fiery Performer

Characteristics of Leo

Leo, the fifth sign of the zodiac, is ruled by the Sun, the center of our solar system and the source of life-giving energy. Known as the "Fiery Performer," Leo embodies creativity, confidence, and a dramatic flair. This fixed fire sign is associated with warmth, generosity, and a strong desire for recognition and admiration. Leo individuals are often seen as charismatic leaders who thrive in the spotlight and exude a radiant energy. In the context of gardening, the Leo influence encourages a vibrant and eye-catching garden that commands attention and admiration.

Key Traits of Leo:

- **Element:** Fire
- **Ruling Planet:** Sun
- **Symbol:** The Lion
- **Modality:** Fixed
- **Attributes:** Confident, creative, generous, dramatic, warm-hearted

Suitable Plants for Leo

Given Leo's radiant and dramatic nature, the best plants for a Leo-influenced garden are those that are bold, vibrant, and command attention. These plants should thrive in full sun and exhibit a showy, regal presence, reflecting the grandeur and warmth of Leo.

Ideal Plants for Leo:

1. **Sunflowers:**
   - **Varieties:** Mammoth, Teddy Bear, Autumn Beauty
   - **Characteristics:** Tall, bright yellow flowers, sun-loving

- **Benefits:** Attracts pollinators, seeds are edible and nutritious

2. **Citrus Trees:**
   - **Varieties:** Lemon, orange, lime, grapefruit
   - **Characteristics:** Evergreen, fragrant flowers, sun-loving
   - **Benefits:** Produces edible fruits, adds fragrance and beauty

3. **Marigolds:**
   - **Varieties:** African marigold, French marigold, Signet marigold
   - **Characteristics:** Bright orange and yellow flowers, sun-loving
   - **Benefits:** Natural pest deterrent, attracts beneficial insects

4. **Zinnias:**
   - **Varieties:** Benary's Giant, Thumbelina, Cut and Come Again
   - **Characteristics:** Brightly colored flowers, sun-loving, easy to grow
   - **Benefits:** Long blooming period, attracts pollinators

5. **Roses:**
   - **Varieties:** Hybrid tea roses, floribunda, climbing roses
   - **Characteristics:** Showy, fragrant blooms, sun-loving
   - **Benefits:** Adds beauty and fragrance, symbol of love and admiration

Best Gardening Practices for Leo

Leo gardeners are known for their enthusiasm and creativity, making them well-suited for creating a garden that is both vibrant and dramatic. Their confident approach ensures that their gardens are well-maintained and visually striking. Here are some best practices tailored to Leo's characteristics:

Planning and Preparation

- **Bold Design:** Leo's love for drama benefits from a bold garden design. Incorporate large, showy plants, and create focal points with dramatic arrangements.
- **Sun Exposure:** Ensure the garden receives full sun, as Leo plants thrive in bright, sunny conditions. Position sun-loving plants where they can receive maximum sunlight.

Planting

- **Group Planting:** Plant in groups to create a striking visual impact. For example, group sunflowers or marigolds together for a bold splash of color.
- **Soil Preparation:** Use Leo's generous nature to enrich the soil with compost and organic matter, ensuring a fertile environment for plant growth.

Maintenance

- **Regular Feeding:** Leo's vibrant energy supports regular feeding of plants. Use a balanced fertilizer to promote healthy growth and abundant blooms.
- **Pruning and Deadheading:** Use Leo's attention to detail to regularly prune and deadhead plants like roses and zinnias to promote continuous blooming and maintain plant health.

Pest and Weed Control

- **Natural Remedies:** Embrace Leo's warm-hearted nature by using natural pest control methods, such as introducing beneficial insects and using organic sprays.

- **Mulching:** Apply mulch to retain moisture, suppress weeds, and improve soil health. Leo gardeners can experiment with decorative mulches to enhance the garden's aesthetic.

Optimal Planting Times for Leo

Timing is crucial for successful gardening. Aligning planting activities with astrological influences can enhance plant growth and overall garden vitality. Here are the optimal planting times for Leo-associated plants:

Sunflowers

- **Optimal Time:** Late spring to early summer
- **Lunar Phase:** Waxing Moon (for strong growth and flowering)

Citrus Trees

- **Optimal Time:** Spring and early fall (depending on the climate)
- **Lunar Phase:** First Quarter Moon (to promote vigorous growth)

Marigolds

- **Optimal Time:** Spring, after the last frost
- **Lunar Phase:** Waxing Gibbous (for strong flowering)

Zinnias

- **Optimal Time:** Spring and early summer
- **Lunar Phase:** Waxing Crescent (to encourage lush foliage)

Roses

- **Optimal Time:** Spring or fall, depending on the climate

- **Lunar Phase:** Waxing Moon (for strong root establishment)

Conclusion

Embracing the fiery and dramatic energy of Leo in your garden can lead to a vibrant and visually striking growing season. By selecting suitable plants like sunflowers, citrus trees, marigolds, zinnias, and roses, and following tailored gardening practices, you can harness the confident spirit of Leo to create a beautiful and bold garden. Aligning planting times with celestial cycles further enhances the connection between the cosmos and your garden, ensuring that your efforts are rewarded with abundant growth and spectacular blooms.

Leo gardeners, with their enthusiasm and creativity, are well-equipped to create a garden that is both vibrant and dramatic, setting the stage for a dazzling and fulfilling gardening experience. By working in harmony with the rhythms of nature, Leo can create a garden that not only thrives but also reflects the grandeur and warmth of the Fiery Performer.

Chapter 6: Virgo: The Earthy Healer

Characteristics of Virgo

Virgo, the sixth sign of the zodiac, is ruled by Mercury, the planet of communication and intellect. Known as the "Earthy Healer," Virgo embodies precision, practicality, and a deep connection to nature's healing properties. This mutable earth sign is associated with meticulous attention to detail, a love for organization, and a strong desire to be of service. Virgo individuals are often seen as analytical, health-conscious, and dedicated to improving their environment. In the context of gardening, the Virgo influence encourages a methodical and health-focused approach to planting and nurturing a garden.

Key Traits of Virgo:

- **Element:** Earth
- **Ruling Planet:** Mercury
- **Symbol:** The Virgin
- **Modality:** Mutable
- **Attributes:** Practical, analytical, detail-oriented, health-conscious, service-oriented

Suitable Plants for Virgo

Given Virgo's practical and health-conscious nature, the best plants for a Virgo-influenced garden are those that have medicinal or nutritional benefits, require meticulous care, and contribute to overall well-being. These plants should reflect Virgo's love for precision and their deep connection to the earth's healing properties.

Ideal Plants for Virgo:

1. **Medicinal Herbs:**
    - **Varieties:** Chamomile, echinacea, lavender, peppermint, rosemary

- **Characteristics:** Healing properties, aromatic, requires careful tending
- **Benefits:** Used for teas, tinctures, and natural remedies

2. **Wheat:**
   - **Varieties:** Hard red wheat, soft red wheat, durum wheat
   - **Characteristics:** Nutrient-rich, requires meticulous planting and harvesting
   - **Benefits:** Source of flour, high in fiber and nutrients

3. **Aloe Vera:**
   - **Varieties:** Aloe barbadensis miller
   - **Characteristics:** Succulent, healing properties, low maintenance
   - **Benefits:** Soothes burns and skin irritations, purifies air

4. **Garlic:**
   - **Varieties:** Hardneck, softneck
   - **Characteristics:** Nutrient-rich, requires careful spacing and timing
   - **Benefits:** Culinary uses, medicinal properties, boosts immune system

5. **Sage:**
   - **Varieties:** Common sage, white sage, pineapple sage
   - **Characteristics:** Aromatic, healing properties, hardy
   - **Benefits:** Culinary uses, medicinal properties, purifies air

Best Gardening Practices for Virgo

Virgo gardeners are known for their meticulous and health-focused approach, making them well-suited for creating a garden that is both orderly and beneficial to health. Their analytical nature ensures that their gardens are well-maintained and productive. Here are some best practices tailored to Virgo's characteristics:

Planning and Preparation

- **Detailed Planning:** Virgo's love for organization benefits from a detailed garden plan. Map out planting locations, companion planting strategies, and a seasonal calendar for planting and harvesting.
- **Soil Testing:** Use Virgo's analytical skills to conduct soil tests and amend the soil as needed to create an optimal growing environment.

Planting

- **Precise Spacing:** Ensure plants are spaced precisely according to their needs. This is especially important for crops like garlic and wheat, which require specific spacing to thrive.
- **Raised Beds and Containers:** Utilize raised beds and containers to maintain control over soil quality and drainage, ensuring plants have the best possible growing conditions.

Maintenance

- **Regular Monitoring:** Virgo's attention to detail drives frequent garden inspections. Regularly check for pests, diseases, and growth progress to address issues promptly.
- **Pruning and Harvesting:** Use Virgo's methodical nature to prune medicinal herbs and harvest crops like garlic and wheat at the optimal times to ensure maximum potency and yield.

Pest and Weed Control

- **Natural Remedies:** Embrace Virgo's health-conscious approach by using natural pest control methods, such as neem oil, diatomaceous earth, and beneficial insects.

- **Weed Management:** Maintain a weed-free garden by regularly hand-weeding and using organic mulches to suppress weed growth and improve soil health.

Optimal Planting Times for Virgo

Timing is crucial for successful gardening. Aligning planting activities with astrological influences can enhance plant growth and overall garden vitality. Here are the optimal planting times for Virgo-associated plants:

Medicinal Herbs

- **Optimal Time:** Spring and early summer
- **Lunar Phase:** Waxing Crescent (to promote lush foliage and healing properties)

Wheat

- **Optimal Time:** Fall for winter wheat, spring for spring wheat
- **Lunar Phase:** New Moon (for quick germination and growth)

Aloe Vera

- **Optimal Time:** Spring and early summer
- **Lunar Phase:** First Quarter Moon (to encourage strong growth)

Garlic

- **Optimal Time:** Fall
- **Lunar Phase:** Waxing Gibbous (for strong root development)

Sage

- **Optimal Time:** Spring

- **Lunar Phase:** Waxing Crescent (to promote healthy foliage)

Conclusion

Embracing the earthy and healing energy of Virgo in your garden can lead to a productive and health-focused growing season. By selecting suitable plants like medicinal herbs, wheat, aloe vera, garlic, and sage, and following tailored gardening practices, you can harness the practical spirit of Virgo to create a garden that is both orderly and beneficial to health. Aligning planting times with celestial cycles further enhances the connection between the cosmos and your garden, ensuring that your efforts are rewarded with abundant growth and potent harvests.

Virgo gardeners, with their meticulous and health-conscious approach, are well-equipped to create a garden that is both productive and healing, setting the stage for a harmonious and fulfilling gardening experience. By working in harmony with the rhythms of nature, Virgo can create a garden that not only thrives but also reflects the practical and healing qualities of the Earthy Healer.

Chapter 7: Libra: The Airy Balancer

Characteristics of Libra

Libra, the seventh sign of the zodiac, is ruled by Venus, the planet of love, beauty, and harmony. Known as the "Airy Balancer," Libra embodies fairness, balance, and an aesthetic sensibility. This cardinal air sign is associated with diplomacy, sociability, and a strong desire for equilibrium and peace. Libra individuals are often seen as charming, cooperative, and dedicated to creating beautiful and harmonious environments. In the context of gardening, the Libra influence encourages a balanced and aesthetically pleasing approach to planting and nurturing a garden.

Key Traits of Libra:

- **Element:** Air
- **Ruling Planet:** Venus
- **Symbol:** The Scales
- **Modality:** Cardinal
- **Attributes:** Harmonious, diplomatic, social, aesthetic, balanced

Suitable Plants for Libra

Given Libra's love for beauty and balance, the best plants for a Libra-influenced garden are those that are visually appealing, promote harmony, and thrive in balanced conditions. These plants should reflect Libra's aesthetic sensibilities and their desire for a harmonious garden environment.

Ideal Plants for Libra:

1. **Ornamental Flowers:**
   - **Varieties:** Roses, hydrangeas, peonies, lilies

- ◦ **Characteristics:** Beautiful blooms, diverse colors, fragrant
- ◦ **Benefits:** Adds beauty and fragrance to the garden, attracts pollinators

2. **Beans:**
   - ◦ **Varieties:** Green beans, runner beans, lima beans
   - ◦ **Characteristics:** Fast-growing, nitrogen-fixing, climbing habit
   - ◦ **Benefits:** Nutrient-rich, improves soil fertility, multiple harvests

3. **Tulips:**
   - ◦ **Varieties:** Single early, double late, parrot tulips
   - ◦ **Characteristics:** Brightly colored blooms, spring-blooming
   - ◦ **Benefits:** Adds early spring color, easy to grow from bulbs

4. **Hostas:**
   - ◦ **Varieties:** Blue hosta, variegated hosta, giant hosta
   - ◦ **Characteristics:** Lush foliage, shade-loving, diverse sizes
   - ◦ **Benefits:** Adds greenery to shady areas, low maintenance

5. **Lavender:**
   - ◦ **Varieties:** English lavender, French lavender, Spanish lavender
   - ◦ **Characteristics:** Aromatic, drought-tolerant, beautiful blooms
   - ◦ **Benefits:** Calming fragrance, medicinal properties, attracts pollinators

Best Gardening Practices for Libra

Libra gardeners are known for their love of harmony and beauty, making them well-suited for creating a garden that is both visually appealing and balanced. Their diplomatic nature ensures that their gardens are well-maintained and pleasing to the eye. Here are some best practices tailored to Libra's characteristics:

Planning and Preparation

- **Symmetrical Design:** Libra's love for balance benefits from a symmetrical garden design. Incorporate balanced arrangements and mirrored plantings to create visual harmony.
- **Color Coordination:** Use Libra's aesthetic sensibility to coordinate colors and textures. Choose plants with complementary colors and foliage to enhance the garden's beauty.

Planting

- **Companion Planting:** Embrace Libra's diplomatic nature by practicing companion planting. Pair compatible plants like beans and lavender to promote mutual growth and pest resistance.
- **Balanced Soil:** Ensure the soil is well-balanced with the right mix of nutrients. Use compost and organic matter to create fertile and well-drained soil.

Maintenance

- **Regular Watering:** Libra's attention to harmony ensures consistent watering. Maintain a regular watering schedule to keep plants healthy and hydrated without over-watering.
- **Pruning and Deadheading:** Use Libra's meticulous nature to regularly prune and deadhead ornamental flowers and beans to promote continuous blooming and healthy growth.

Pest and Weed Control

- **Natural Remedies:** Embrace Libra's love for harmony by using natural pest control methods, such as neem oil, companion planting, and introducing beneficial insects.
- **Mulching:** Apply mulch to retain moisture, suppress weeds, and improve soil health. Libra gardeners can choose decorative mulches to enhance the garden's aesthetic.

Optimal Planting Times for Libra

Timing is crucial for successful gardening. Aligning planting activities with astrological influences can enhance plant growth and overall garden vitality. Here are the optimal planting times for Libra-associated plants:

Ornamental Flowers

- **Optimal Time:** Spring and fall
- **Lunar Phase:** Waxing Moon (for strong growth and blooming)

Beans

- **Optimal Time:** Late spring to early summer
- **Lunar Phase:** Waxing Crescent (to promote lush foliage and growth)

Tulips

- **Optimal Time:** Fall
- **Lunar Phase:** Waning Moon (for strong root establishment)

Hostas

- **Optimal Time:** Spring and fall
- **Lunar Phase:** Waxing Crescent (to encourage lush foliage)

Lavender

- **Optimal Time:** Late spring to early summer
- **Lunar Phase:** First Quarter Moon (to promote strong growth)

Conclusion

Embracing the airy and balanced energy of Libra in your garden can lead to a harmonious and visually stunning growing season. By selecting suitable plants like ornamental flowers, beans, tulips, hostas, and lavender, and following tailored gardening practices, you can harness the balanced spirit of Libra to create a garden that is both beautiful and harmonious. Aligning planting times with celestial cycles further enhances the connection between the cosmos and your garden, ensuring that your efforts are rewarded with abundant growth and visual appeal.

Libra gardeners, with their love for harmony and beauty, are well-equipped to create a garden that is both balanced and aesthetically pleasing, setting the stage for a serene and fulfilling gardening experience. By working in harmony with the rhythms of nature, Libra can create a garden that not only thrives but also reflects the balanced and harmonious qualities of the Airy Balancer.

Chapter 8: Scorpio: The Watery Transformer
Characteristics of Scorpio

Scorpio, the eighth sign of the zodiac, is ruled by Pluto, the planet of transformation, and Mars, the planet of action and desire. Known as the "Watery Transformer," Scorpio embodies intensity, depth, and a powerful transformative energy. This fixed water sign is associated with mystery, passion, and an unwavering determination. Scorpio individuals are often seen as resourceful, resilient, and deeply intuitive, making them adept at uncovering hidden potentials and bringing about profound changes. In the context of gardening, the Scorpio influence encourages a transformative and deeply nurturing approach to planting and nurturing a garden.

Key Traits of Scorpio:

- **Element:** Water
- **Ruling Planets:** Pluto and Mars
- **Symbol:** The Scorpion
- **Modality:** Fixed
- **Attributes:** Intense, resourceful, passionate, transformative, intuitive

Suitable Plants for Scorpio

Given Scorpio's intense and transformative nature, the best plants for a Scorpio-influenced garden are those that thrive in rich, fertile soils, often have deep or mysterious qualities, and are capable of withstanding challenging conditions. These plants should reflect Scorpio's ability to transform and thrive in adversity.

Ideal Plants for Scorpio:

1. **Nightshades:**
    ◦ **Varieties:** Tomatoes, eggplants, bell peppers, potatoes
    ◦ **Characteristics:** Deeply rooted, often vibrant colors, requires rich soil
    ◦ **Benefits:** Nutrient-rich, versatile in culinary uses
2. **Garlic:**
    ◦ **Varieties:** Hardneck, softneck
    ◦ **Characteristics:** Nutrient-rich, requires careful spacing and timing
    ◦ **Benefits:** Culinary uses, medicinal properties, boosts immune system
3. **Blackberries:**
    ◦ **Varieties:** Thornless, trailing, erect
    ◦ **Characteristics:** Hardy, deep-rooted, produces dark, rich berries
    ◦ **Benefits:** High in antioxidants, versatile in culinary uses
4. **Hellebores:**
    ◦ **Varieties:** Lenten rose, Christmas rose
    ◦ **Characteristics:** Evergreen, early bloomers, often dark flowers
    ◦ **Benefits:** Adds winter interest, shade-loving, long-lasting blooms
5. **Wormwood (Artemisia):**
    ◦ **Varieties:** Silver mound, sweet wormwood, tarragon
    ◦ **Characteristics:** Aromatic, hardy, silvery foliage
    ◦ **Benefits:** Medicinal uses, natural pest deterrent, ornamental

Best Gardening Practices for Scorpio

Scorpio gardeners are known for their intensity and resilience, making them well-suited for creating a garden that is both deeply transformative and nurturing. Their intuitive approach ensures that their gardens are well-maintained and capable of thriving under challenging conditions. Here are some best practices tailored to Scorpio's characteristics:

Planning and Preparation

- **Deep Soil Preparation:** Scorpio's love for depth benefits from preparing the soil thoroughly. Ensure the soil is deeply tilled and enriched with compost and organic matter to create a fertile environment.
- **Mulching:** Use Scorpio's resourcefulness to apply mulch, which helps retain moisture, suppress weeds, and improve soil health.

Planting

- **Rich, Fertile Soil:** Scorpio's plants thrive in rich, fertile soils. Incorporate plenty of organic matter and compost to ensure the soil is nutrient-dense.
- **Companion Planting:** Use companion planting strategies to enhance plant growth and protect against pests. Pairing garlic with nightshades, for example, can help deter pests and improve soil health.

Maintenance

- **Consistent Watering:** Scorpio's intensity ensures regular and deep watering, especially for plants like nightshades and blackberries that require consistent moisture. Avoid over-watering by monitoring soil moisture levels.

- **Pruning and Training:** Use Scorpio's meticulous nature to regularly prune and train plants like blackberries to promote healthy growth and maximize fruit production.

Pest and Weed Control

- **Natural Remedies:** Embrace Scorpio's intuitive approach by using natural pest control methods, such as neem oil, diatomaceous earth, and beneficial insects. Companion planting with wormwood can also help deter pests.
- **Weed Management:** Maintain a weed-free garden by regularly hand-weeding and using mulch to suppress weed growth and improve soil health.

Optimal Planting Times for Scorpio

Timing is crucial for successful gardening. Aligning planting activities with astrological influences can enhance plant growth and overall garden vitality. Here are the optimal planting times for Scorpio-associated plants:

Nightshades

- **Optimal Time:** Late spring to early summer
- **Lunar Phase:** Waxing Moon (for strong growth and fruiting)

Garlic

- **Optimal Time:** Fall
- **Lunar Phase:** Waning Moon (for strong root establishment)

Blackberries

- **Optimal Time:** Spring
- **Lunar Phase:** Waxing Crescent (to promote strong growth)

Hellebores

- **Optimal Time:** Fall
- **Lunar Phase:** First Quarter Moon (to encourage early blooming)

Wormwood (Artemisia)

- **Optimal Time:** Spring
- **Lunar Phase:** Waxing Gibbous (for strong foliage development)

Conclusion

Embracing the watery and transformative energy of Scorpio in your garden can lead to a deeply nurturing and resilient growing season. By selecting suitable plants like nightshades, garlic, blackberries, hellebores, and wormwood, and following tailored gardening practices, you can harness the intense spirit of Scorpio to create a garden that is both transformative and thriving. Aligning planting times with celestial cycles further enhances the connection between the cosmos and your garden, ensuring that your efforts are rewarded with abundant growth and successful harvests.

Scorpio gardeners, with their intensity and resilience, are well-equipped to create a garden that is both deeply nurturing and capable of withstanding challenges, setting the stage for a powerful and fulfilling gardening experience. By working in harmony with the rhythms of nature, Scorpio can create a garden that not only thrives but also reflects the transformative and mysterious qualities of the Watery Transformer.

Chapter 9: Sagittarius: The Fiery Explorer
Characteristics of Sagittarius

Sagittarius, the ninth sign of the zodiac, is ruled by Jupiter, the planet of expansion, wisdom, and adventure. Known as the "Fiery Explorer," Sagittarius embodies curiosity, optimism, and a thirst for knowledge and new experiences. This mutable fire sign is associated with exploration, freedom, and a boundless enthusiasm for life. Sagittarius individuals are often seen as adventurous, philosophical, and open-minded, making them adept at experimenting with new gardening techniques and exotic plants. In the context of gardening, the Sagittarius influence encourages a bold and expansive approach to planting and nurturing a garden.

Key Traits of Sagittarius:

- **Element:** Fire
- **Ruling Planet:** Jupiter
- **Symbol:** The Archer
- **Modality:** Mutable
- **Attributes:** Adventurous, optimistic, curious, philosophical, expansive

Suitable Plants for Sagittarius

Given Sagittarius' adventurous and expansive nature, the best plants for a Sagittarius-influenced garden are those that are exotic, thrive in diverse conditions, and often produce abundant yields. These plants should reflect Sagittarius' love for exploration and their desire to cultivate a garden that is both diverse and bountiful.

Ideal Plants for Sagittarius:

1. **Exotic Plants:**
   - **Varieties:** Bird of Paradise, hibiscus, passionflower, bougainvillea
   - **Characteristics:** Vibrant, tropical, often large and showy blooms
   - **Benefits:** Adds a touch of the exotic, attracts pollinators, enhances garden diversity

2. **Fruit Trees:**
   - **Varieties:** Fig, pomegranate, citrus, banana
   - **Characteristics:** Produces edible fruits, often requires full sun and rich soil
   - **Benefits:** Provides fresh fruit, adds beauty and shade to the garden

3. **Herbs:**
   - **Varieties:** Lemongrass, ginger, turmeric, rosemary
   - **Characteristics:** Aromatic, medicinal properties, often used in diverse cuisines
   - **Benefits:** Culinary and medicinal uses, enhances garden fragrance

4. **Climbing Plants:**
   - **Varieties:** Kiwi, grapevine, jasmine, wisteria
   - **Characteristics:** Fast-growing, often produces flowers or fruits, requires support structures
   - **Benefits:** Adds vertical interest, provides shade and privacy, attracts pollinators

5. **Colorful Perennials:**
   - **Varieties:** Daylilies, coneflowers, salvia, lantana
   - **Characteristics:** Vibrant blooms, hardy, attracts pollinators

◦ **Benefits:** Long blooming period, low maintenance, enhances garden color

Best Gardening Practices for Sagittarius

Sagittarius gardeners are known for their enthusiasm and adventurous spirit, making them well-suited for experimenting with diverse plants and gardening techniques. Their expansive approach ensures that their gardens are dynamic and bountiful. Here are some best practices tailored to Sagittarius' characteristics:

Planning and Preparation

- **Diverse Planting:** Sagittarius' love for diversity benefits from a garden plan that includes a wide variety of plants. Incorporate exotic plants, fruit trees, herbs, climbers, and perennials to create a rich and diverse garden.
- **Soil Enrichment:** Use Sagittarius' expansive nature to enrich the soil with compost and organic matter, ensuring a fertile environment for plant growth.

Planting

- **Wide Spacing:** Ensure plants have ample space to grow and expand. Fruit trees and climbing plants, in particular, require adequate spacing to thrive.
- **Support Structures:** Use support structures for climbing plants to encourage vertical growth and maximize garden space.

Maintenance

- **Regular Feeding:** Sagittarius' enthusiasm supports regular feeding of plants. Use a balanced fertilizer to promote healthy growth and abundant blooms or fruits.

- **Pruning and Training:** Use Sagittarius' adventurous nature to regularly prune and train plants like fruit trees and climbers to maintain healthy growth and maximize yields.

Pest and Weed Control

- **Natural Remedies:** Embrace Sagittarius' philosophical approach by using natural pest control methods, such as neem oil, diatomaceous earth, and beneficial insects.
- **Weed Management:** Maintain a weed-free garden by regularly hand-weeding and using organic mulches to suppress weed growth and improve soil health.

Optimal Planting Times for Sagittarius

Timing is crucial for successful gardening. Aligning planting activities with astrological influences can enhance plant growth and overall garden vitality. Here are the optimal planting times for Sagittarius-associated plants:

Exotic Plants

- **Optimal Time:** Late spring to early summer
- **Lunar Phase:** Waxing Moon (for strong growth and flowering)

Fruit Trees

- **Optimal Time:** Spring and early fall (depending on the climate)
- **Lunar Phase:** First Quarter Moon (to promote vigorous growth)

Herbs

- **Optimal Time:** Spring and early summer
- **Lunar Phase:** Waxing Crescent (to promote lush foliage)

Climbing Plants

- **Optimal Time:** Spring
- **Lunar Phase:** Waxing Gibbous (for strong growth and flowering)

Colorful Perennials

- **Optimal Time:** Spring and early summer
- **Lunar Phase:** Waxing Crescent (to encourage lush foliage)

Conclusion

Embracing the fiery and adventurous energy of Sagittarius in your garden can lead to a dynamic and bountiful growing season. By selecting suitable plants like exotic plants, fruit trees, herbs, climbing plants, and colorful perennials, and following tailored gardening practices, you can harness the expansive spirit of Sagittarius to create a garden that is both diverse and productive. Aligning planting times with celestial cycles further enhances the connection between the cosmos and your garden, ensuring that your efforts are rewarded with abundant growth and successful harvests.

Sagittarius gardeners, with their enthusiasm and curiosity, are well-equipped to experiment with diverse plants and techniques, setting the stage for an exciting and fulfilling gardening experience. By working in harmony with the rhythms of nature, Sagittarius can create a garden that not only thrives but also reflects the adventurous and expansive qualities of the Fiery Explorer.

Chapter 10: Capricorn: The Earthy Builder
Characteristics of Capricorn

Capricorn, the tenth sign of the zodiac, is ruled by Saturn, the planet of discipline, structure, and perseverance. Known as the "Earthy Builder," Capricorn embodies practicality, ambition, and a strong work ethic. This cardinal earth sign is associated with determination, responsibility, and a methodical approach to achieving long-term goals. Capricorn individuals are often seen as reliable, disciplined, and patient, making them adept at planning and executing well-structured and productive gardens. In the context of gardening, the Capricorn influence encourages a strategic and disciplined approach to planting and nurturing a garden.

Key Traits of Capricorn:

- **Element:** Earth
- **Ruling Planet:** Saturn
- **Symbol:** The Goat
- **Modality:** Cardinal
- **Attributes:** Practical, disciplined, ambitious, methodical, patient

Suitable Plants for Capricorn

Given Capricorn's practical and disciplined nature, the best plants for a Capricorn-influenced garden are those that require long-term care, provide substantial yields, and contribute to a well-structured garden environment. These plants should reflect Capricorn's dedication and ability to thrive in challenging conditions.

Ideal Plants for Capricorn:

1. **Trees:**
   - **Varieties:** Oak, maple, apple, pear
   - **Characteristics:** Long-living, requires deep soil, provides shade and structure
   - **Benefits:** Produces fruit (for fruit trees), adds beauty and structure, provides long-term benefits
2. **Root Vegetables:**
   - **Varieties:** Carrots, potatoes, beets, turnips
   - **Characteristics:** Nutrient-rich, requires deep soil, long growing season
   - **Benefits:** High in vitamins and minerals, long storage life, essential for winter sustenance
3. **Evergreen Shrubs:**
   - **Varieties:** Boxwood, holly, juniper, yew
   - **Characteristics:** Hardy, provides year-round greenery, low maintenance
   - **Benefits:** Adds structure and privacy, improves garden aesthetics
4. **Herbs:**
   - **Varieties:** Rosemary, sage, thyme, oregano
   - **Characteristics:** Hardy, aromatic, perennial
   - **Benefits:** Culinary and medicinal uses, improves garden fragrance, attracts pollinators
5. **Perennial Vegetables:**
   - **Varieties:** Asparagus, rhubarb, artichokes
   - **Characteristics:** Long-lived, requires patience for first harvest, high yield over time
   - **Benefits:** Provides annual harvests, high in nutrients, improves soil structure

Best Gardening Practices for Capricorn

Capricorn gardeners are known for their discipline and ambition, making them well-suited for creating a garden that is both productive and well-structured. Their methodical approach ensures that their gardens are well-maintained and capable of providing substantial yields. Here are some best practices tailored to Capricorn's characteristics:

Planning and Preparation

- **Long-Term Planning:** Capricorn's love for structure benefits from a long-term garden plan. Include perennial plants, trees, and root vegetables that will provide benefits for years to come.
- **Soil Preparation:** Use Capricorn's methodical nature to prepare the soil thoroughly. Ensure the soil is deeply tilled and enriched with compost and organic matter to create a fertile environment.

Planting

- **Deep Planting:** Ensure plants with deep root systems, like trees and root vegetables, are planted in well-prepared soil to encourage strong root development.
- **Structured Layout:** Use Capricorn's practical approach to create a structured garden layout. Include paths, raised beds, and clear boundaries to maintain order and ease of access.

Maintenance

- **Consistent Care:** Capricorn's disciplined nature ensures regular and consistent care. Water plants deeply and regularly, especially during dry spells, and monitor for signs of pests and diseases.
- **Pruning and Training:** Use Capricorn's attention to detail to regularly prune and train trees and shrubs to maintain their shape and promote healthy growth.

Pest and Weed Control

- **Natural Remedies:** Embrace Capricorn's practical approach by using natural pest control methods, such as neem oil, diatomaceous earth, and beneficial insects.
- **Weed Management:** Maintain a weed-free garden by regularly hand-weeding and using mulch to suppress weed growth and improve soil health.

Optimal Planting Times for Capricorn

Timing is crucial for successful gardening. Aligning planting activities with astrological influences can enhance plant growth and overall garden vitality. Here are the optimal planting times for Capricorn-associated plants:

Trees

- **Optimal Time:** Late fall to early spring (depending on the climate)
- **Lunar Phase:** Waxing Moon (for strong root establishment)

Root Vegetables

- **Optimal Time:** Early spring and late summer
- **Lunar Phase:** New Moon (for quick germination and growth)

Evergreen Shrubs

- **Optimal Time:** Early spring and late fall
- **Lunar Phase:** Waxing Crescent (to promote lush foliage)

Herbs

- **Optimal Time:** Spring and early summer

- **Lunar Phase:** Waxing Crescent (to promote lush foliage)

Perennial Vegetables

- **Optimal Time:** Early spring
- **Lunar Phase:** First Quarter Moon (to promote strong growth)

Conclusion

Embracing the earthy and disciplined energy of Capricorn in your garden can lead to a productive and well-structured growing season. By selecting suitable plants like trees, root vegetables, evergreen shrubs, herbs, and perennial vegetables, and following tailored gardening practices, you can harness the practical spirit of Capricorn to create a garden that is both orderly and bountiful. Aligning planting times with celestial cycles further enhances the connection between the cosmos and your garden, ensuring that your efforts are rewarded with abundant growth and successful harvests.

Capricorn gardeners, with their discipline and ambition, are well-equipped to create a garden that is both productive and well-maintained, setting the stage for a fulfilling and sustainable gardening experience. By working in harmony with the rhythms of nature, Capricorn can create a garden that not only thrives but also reflects the practical and structured qualities of the Earthy Builder.

Chapter 11: Aquarius: The Airy Innovator
Characteristics of Aquarius

Aquarius, the eleventh sign of the zodiac, is ruled by Uranus, the planet of innovation, and Saturn, the planet of structure. Known as the "Airy Innovator," Aquarius embodies originality, forward-thinking, and a desire for change and progress. This fixed air sign is associated with independence, humanitarianism, and a visionary approach to life. Aquarius individuals are often seen as inventive, unconventional, and ahead of their time, making them adept at experimenting with new gardening techniques and unusual plants. In the context of gardening, the Aquarius influence encourages a creative and innovative approach to planting and nurturing a garden.

Key Traits of Aquarius:

- **Element:** Air
- **Ruling Planets:** Uranus and Saturn
- **Symbol:** The Water Bearer
- **Modality:** Fixed
- **Attributes:** Innovative, independent, forward-thinking, humanitarian, visionary

Suitable Plants for Aquarius

Given Aquarius' innovative and unconventional nature, the best plants for an Aquarius-influenced garden are those that are unique, rare, and adaptable to various conditions. These plants should reflect Aquarius' love for experimentation and their desire to create a garden that is both distinctive and forward-thinking.

Ideal Plants for Aquarius:

1. **Unusual or Rare Plants:**
   - **Varieties:** Pitcher plants, Venus flytraps, dragon fruit, blue roses
   - **Characteristics:** Unique appearance, often requires specific conditions
   - **Benefits:** Adds an element of surprise and novelty to the garden
2. **Air Plants (Tillandsia):**
   - **Varieties:** Tillandsia ionantha, Tillandsia xerographica, Tillandsia cyanea
   - **Characteristics:** Epiphytic, requires no soil, low maintenance
   - **Benefits:** Easy to care for, versatile in display options, improves air quality
3. **Succulents:**
   - **Varieties:** Echeveria, aloe vera, jade plant, haworthia
   - **Characteristics:** Drought-tolerant, unique shapes, low maintenance
   - **Benefits:** Requires minimal water, easy to propagate, adds texture and form
4. **Vertical Garden Plants:**
   - **Varieties:** Ferns, pothos, philodendrons, ivy
   - **Characteristics:** Adaptable to vertical growth, requires support structures
   - **Benefits:** Maximizes space, improves air quality, adds greenery to vertical surfaces
5. **Edible Perennials:**
   - **Varieties:** Asparagus, artichokes, rhubarb, sea kale

- ◦ **Characteristics:** Long-lived, requires patience for first harvest, high yield over time
- ◦ **Benefits:** Provides annual harvests, high in nutrients, contributes to sustainable gardening

Best Gardening Practices for Aquarius

Aquarius gardeners are known for their creativity and forward-thinking approach, making them well-suited for experimenting with innovative gardening techniques and unique plants. Their independent nature ensures that their gardens are distinctive and filled with novel ideas. Here are some best practices tailored to Aquarius' characteristics:

Planning and Preparation

- **Innovative Design:** Aquarius' love for originality benefits from a creative garden design. Incorporate vertical gardens, unusual plant arrangements, and innovative structures to create a unique garden space.
- **Soil and Environment:** Use Aquarius' forward-thinking nature to prepare the garden environment. Ensure well-draining soil for succulents and air plants, and create microclimates for rare and unusual plants.

Planting

- **Diverse Planting:** Ensure a diverse mix of plants that reflect Aquarius' innovative spirit. Include unusual plants, air plants, succulents, vertical garden plants, and edible perennials to create a varied and interesting garden.
- **Creative Containers:** Use creative containers and display options for air plants and succulents. Consider hanging displays, wall-mounted planters, and unconventional pots.

Maintenance

- **Watering:** Aquarius' adaptability supports innovative watering techniques. Use drip irrigation for succulents and unusual plants that require specific watering conditions, and mist air plants regularly.
- **Pruning and Care:** Use Aquarius' meticulous nature to regularly prune and care for vertical garden plants and edible perennials. This promotes healthy growth and maximizes yields.

Pest and Weed Control

- **Natural Remedies:** Embrace Aquarius' humanitarian approach by using natural pest control methods, such as neem oil, diatomaceous earth, and beneficial insects.
- **Weed Management:** Maintain a weed-free garden by regularly hand-weeding and using mulch to suppress weed growth and improve soil health.

Optimal Planting Times for Aquarius

Timing is crucial for successful gardening. Aligning planting activities with astrological influences can enhance plant growth and overall garden vitality. Here are the optimal planting times for Aquarius-associated plants:

Unusual or Rare Plants

- **Optimal Time:** Late spring to early summer
- **Lunar Phase:** Waxing Moon (for strong growth and flowering)

Air Plants (Tillandsia)

- **Optimal Time:** Spring and early summer

• **Lunar Phase:** Waxing Crescent (to promote lush foliage)

Succulents

- **Optimal Time:** Spring
- **Lunar Phase:** Waxing Crescent (to encourage strong growth)

Vertical Garden Plants

- **Optimal Time:** Spring and early summer
- **Lunar Phase:** First Quarter Moon (to promote vigorous growth)

Edible Perennials

- **Optimal Time:** Early spring
- **Lunar Phase:** Waxing Gibbous (for strong root establishment)

Conclusion

Embracing the airy and innovative energy of Aquarius in your garden can lead to a dynamic and forward-thinking growing season. By selecting suitable plants like unusual or rare plants, air plants, succulents, vertical garden plants, and edible perennials, and following tailored gardening practices, you can harness the inventive spirit of Aquarius to create a garden that is both unique and productive. Aligning planting times with celestial cycles further enhances the connection between the cosmos and your garden, ensuring that your efforts are rewarded with abundant growth and successful harvests.

Aquarius gardeners, with their creativity and forward-thinking approach, are well-equipped to experiment with novel plants and techniques, setting the stage for an exciting and fulfilling gardening experience. By working in harmony with the rhythms of nature, Aquarius can create a garden that not only thrives but also reflects the innovative and visionary qualities of the Airy Innovator.

Chapter 12: Pisces: The Watery Dreamer
Characteristics of Pisces

Pisces, the twelfth sign of the zodiac, is ruled by Neptune, the planet of dreams, intuition, and spirituality, and Jupiter, the planet of expansion. Known as the "Watery Dreamer," Pisces embodies compassion, creativity, and a deep connection to the emotional and spiritual realms. This mutable water sign is associated with empathy, sensitivity, and a rich inner world. Pisces individuals are often seen as imaginative, intuitive, and compassionate, making them adept at creating serene and magical garden spaces. In the context of gardening, the Pisces influence encourages a dreamy and tranquil approach to planting and nurturing a garden.

Key Traits of Pisces:

- **Element:** Water
- **Ruling Planets:** Neptune and Jupiter
- **Symbol:** The Fish
- **Modality:** Mutable
- **Attributes:** Compassionate, intuitive, imaginative, sensitive, spiritual

Suitable Plants for Pisces

Given Pisces' dreamy and intuitive nature, the best plants for a Pisces-influenced garden are those that thrive in moist or aquatic environments, have a calming presence, and often evoke a sense of tranquility and beauty. These plants should reflect Pisces' love for water and their desire to create a serene and magical garden space.

Ideal Plants for Pisces:

1. **Aquatic Plants:**
    - **Varieties:** Water lilies, lotus, water hyacinth, duckweed
    - **Characteristics:** Thrives in water, beautiful blooms, floating or submerged

- **Benefits:** Enhances water features, provides habitat for aquatic life, adds beauty and tranquility

2. **Lilies:**
   - **Varieties:** Calla lilies, daylilies, Asiatic lilies, Oriental lilies
   - **Characteristics:** Large, showy blooms, prefers moist soil, fragrant
   - **Benefits:** Adds color and fragrance, attracts pollinators, long-lasting blooms

3. **Ferns:**
   - **Varieties:** Boston fern, maidenhair fern, sword fern, staghorn fern
   - **Characteristics:** Lush green foliage, prefers shade and moisture
   - **Benefits:** Adds greenery to shady areas, improves air quality, low maintenance

4. **Hostas:**
   - **Varieties:** Blue hosta, variegated hosta, giant hosta
   - **Characteristics:** Shade-loving, diverse sizes and colors, low maintenance
   - **Benefits:** Adds texture and color to shady areas, low maintenance, improves garden aesthetics

5. **Ivy:**
   - **Varieties:** English ivy, Algerian ivy, Persian ivy
   - **Characteristics:** Climbing or trailing habit, evergreen, hardy
   - **Benefits:** Adds greenery to vertical spaces, provides ground cover, improves air quality

Best Gardening Practices for Pisces

Pisces gardeners are known for their creativity and intuitive approach, making them well-suited for creating serene and magical garden spaces. Their empathetic nature ensures that their gardens are nurturing and capable of providing a peaceful retreat. Here are some best practices tailored to Pisces' characteristics:

Planning and Preparation

- **Tranquil Design:** Pisces' love for serenity benefits from a tranquil garden design. Incorporate water features, shaded areas, and soft, flowing lines to create a peaceful garden space.
- **Soil and Environment:** Use Pisces' intuitive nature to prepare the garden environment. Ensure well-draining soil for lilies and ferns, and create aquatic habitats for water plants.

Planting

- **Moisture-Retentive Soil:** Ensure plants with high moisture needs, like lilies and ferns, are planted in moisture-retentive soil. Incorporate organic matter and mulch to retain soil moisture.
- **Water Features:** Incorporate water features, such as ponds or water gardens, to create habitats for aquatic plants and enhance the garden's tranquility.

Maintenance

- **Regular Watering:** Pisces' sensitivity supports regular and deep watering, especially for plants that thrive in moist conditions. Avoid over-watering by monitoring soil moisture levels.
- **Pruning and Care:** Use Pisces' empathetic nature to regularly prune and care for ferns, hostas, and ivy to maintain their health and appearance.

Pest and Weed Control

- **Natural Remedies:** Embrace Pisces' compassionate approach by using natural pest control methods, such as neem oil, diatomaceous earth, and beneficial insects.
- **Weed Management:** Maintain a weed-free garden by regularly hand-weeding and using mulch to suppress weed growth and improve soil health.

Optimal Planting Times for Pisces

Timing is crucial for successful gardening. Aligning planting activities with astrological influences can enhance plant growth and overall garden vitality. Here are the optimal planting times for Pisces-associated plants:

Aquatic Plants

- **Optimal Time:** Late spring to early summer
- **Lunar Phase:** Waxing Moon (for strong growth and flowering)

Lilies

- **Optimal Time:** Spring and early summer
- **Lunar Phase:** Waxing Crescent (to promote lush foliage)

Ferns

- **Optimal Time:** Spring and early summer
- **Lunar Phase:** Waxing Crescent (to encourage strong growth)

Hostas

- **Optimal Time:** Spring and early summer

- **Lunar Phase:** Waxing Crescent (to promote lush foliage)

Ivy

- **Optimal Time:** Spring and early fall
- **Lunar Phase:** Waxing Crescent (to encourage strong growth)

Conclusion

Embracing the watery and dreamy energy of Pisces in your garden can lead to a serene and tranquil growing season. By selecting suitable plants like aquatic plants, lilies, ferns, hostas, and ivy, and following tailored gardening practices, you can harness the compassionate spirit of Pisces to create a garden that is both peaceful and magical. Aligning planting times with celestial cycles further enhances the connection between the cosmos and your garden, ensuring that your efforts are rewarded with abundant growth and successful harvests.

Pisces gardeners, with their creativity and intuitive approach, are well-equipped to create a garden that is both nurturing and serene, setting the stage for a peaceful and fulfilling gardening experience. By working in harmony with the rhythms of nature, Pisces can create a garden that not only thrives but also reflects the dreamy and compassionate qualities of the Watery Dreamer.

Part 2: The Planets and Gardening

Chapter 13: The Sun: The Life Giver

Role of the Sun in Gardening

The Sun, at the center of our solar system, is the primary source of energy for life on Earth. In gardening, the Sun plays a crucial role as the "Life Giver," providing the light and warmth necessary for photosynthesis, which is the process by which plants convert light energy into chemical energy. This process fuels plant growth, development, and reproduction. Understanding the role of the Sun in gardening is essential for optimizing plant health and maximizing garden productivity.

Key Functions of the Sun in Gardening:

- **Photosynthesis:** Enables plants to produce food by converting light energy into sugars.
- **Temperature Regulation:** Warms the soil and air, promoting seed germination and plant growth.
- **Circadian Rhythms:** Regulates plant biological clocks, influencing flowering, leaf expansion, and other growth processes.
- **Vitamin D Production:** Sunlight exposure helps some plants produce essential vitamins and nutrients.

How Solar Energy Affects Plant Growth

Solar energy is critical to several stages of plant growth and development. The amount and quality of sunlight a plant receives can significantly impact its health and productivity. Here are the primary ways solar energy affects plant growth:

Photosynthesis

Photosynthesis is the foundation of plant growth. It involves the absorption of sunlight by chlorophyll in plant cells, which converts carbon dioxide and water into glucose and oxygen. The glucose provides energy for plant growth and development, while the oxygen is released into the atmosphere.

Seed Germination

Sunlight warms the soil, creating optimal conditions for seed germination. Some seeds require direct sunlight to germinate, while others need darkness. Understanding the light requirements of different seeds helps gardeners ensure successful germination.

Growth and Development

Plants grow and develop in response to sunlight. Adequate sunlight encourages robust growth, strong stems, and healthy foliage. Insufficient light can lead to leggy, weak plants with poor coloration and reduced productivity.

Flowering and Fruiting

Sunlight is essential for flowering and fruiting. Many plants require a specific amount of light exposure to trigger blooming and fruit production. Long days (more sunlight) can promote flowering in long-day plants, while short days (less sunlight) are necessary for short-day plants.

Circadian Rhythms

Plants have internal biological clocks that are regulated by light and dark cycles. These circadian rhythms influence various processes, including leaf movement, nutrient uptake, and the opening and closing of stomata (pores on leaves).

Aligning Planting Schedules with Solar Cycles

To maximize garden productivity and plant health, it is crucial to align planting schedules with solar cycles. Understanding the seasonal changes in sunlight and how they affect plant growth helps gardeners plan their activities effectively.

Seasonal Sunlight Changes

The amount and intensity of sunlight vary with the seasons. Spring and summer provide longer days and more intense sunlight, ideal for most plant growth. Fall and winter have shorter days and less intense sunlight, which can slow down plant growth.

Planting by Season

- **Spring:** A time of renewal and growth. Start planting cool-season crops like lettuce, spinach, and peas early in the season. As temperatures rise, transition to warm-season crops like tomatoes, peppers, and beans.
- **Summer:** The peak growing season with abundant sunlight. Focus on heat-loving plants such as corn, cucumbers, and sunflowers. Ensure consistent watering and mulching to retain soil moisture.
- **Fall:** A time for planting cool-season crops again, such as broccoli, kale, and carrots. Take advantage of the still-warm soil to establish new perennials and bulbs.
- **Winter:** In mild climates, continue growing hardy vegetables like garlic, onions, and winter greens. Use cold frames or greenhouses to extend the growing season in colder areas.

Solar Exposure and Plant Placement

Understanding the specific light requirements of plants helps gardeners place them in optimal locations. Here are some general guidelines:

- **Full Sun Plants:** Require at least 6-8 hours of direct sunlight daily. Examples include tomatoes, peppers, and sunflowers.
- **Partial Sun/Partial Shade Plants:** Thrive with 3-6 hours of direct sunlight. Examples include lettuce, spinach, and hostas.
- **Shade Plants:** Prefer less than 3 hours of direct sunlight or filtered light. Examples include ferns, impatiens, and many woodland plants.

Sunlight and Microclimates

Microclimates within a garden can affect sunlight exposure. Buildings, trees, and other structures can create shaded areas, while south-facing slopes receive more sunlight. Utilize microclimates to match plant light requirements with the available sunlight in different garden areas.

Practical Tips for Maximizing Solar Energy in the Garden

To make the most of the Sun's energy, gardeners can implement several practical strategies:

Garden Layout

Design the garden layout to maximize sunlight exposure. Place tall plants or structures on the north side to avoid shading shorter plants. Use reflective surfaces like white walls or light-colored mulch to increase light availability.

Season Extension

Extend the growing season by using cold frames, hoop houses, or greenhouses. These structures trap solar energy, keeping plants warm and protected from frost during early spring and late fall.

Pruning and Thinning

Regularly prune and thin plants to ensure adequate light penetration and air circulation. This practice reduces shading and promotes healthier, more productive plants.

Solar-Powered Garden Tools

Incorporate solar-powered garden tools and equipment, such as solar water pumps and lighting, to reduce reliance on traditional energy sources and promote sustainability.

Monitoring and Adjusting

Monitor sunlight exposure throughout the growing season and adjust plant placement or protective measures as needed. Use sun charts or apps to track daily and seasonal sunlight patterns in the garden.

Conclusion

Understanding the critical role of the Sun in gardening and how solar energy affects plant growth is essential for creating a thriving garden. By aligning planting schedules with solar cycles and optimizing garden layout and practices, gardeners can harness the full potential of the Sun's life-giving energy. The Sun, as the Life Giver, provides the foundation for all plant growth, ensuring a bountiful and healthy garden when utilized effectively.

Embrace the power of the Sun in your gardening endeavors, and let its energy guide you in creating a garden that is vibrant, productive, and in harmony with the natural rhythms of the cosmos. With thoughtful planning and attention to solar cycles, you can cultivate a garden that flourishes under the nurturing light of the Sun.

Chapter 14: The Moon: The Emotional Influencer
Role of the Moon in Gardening

The Moon, with its powerful gravitational pull and cyclical phases, plays a significant role in gardening. Known as the "Emotional Influencer," the Moon affects water movement on Earth, influencing tides, groundwater levels, and even the moisture content in plants. Gardeners have long used lunar phases to guide planting, watering, and harvesting activities, believing that working in harmony with the Moon's cycles can enhance plant growth and productivity.

Key Functions of the Moon in Gardening:

- **Gravitational Pull:** Influences water movement, affecting soil moisture and plant sap flow.
- **Lunar Phases:** Guides planting, watering, and harvesting schedules.
- **Biological Rhythms:** Regulates plant growth cycles and nutrient uptake.

Lunar Phases and Their Impact on Gardening

The Moon goes through eight distinct phases in its 29.5-day lunar cycle. Each phase has unique gravitational and light effects that influence various gardening activities. Understanding these phases helps gardeners optimize their efforts to achieve better results.

New Moon

- **Characteristics:** The Moon is not visible from Earth as it is positioned between the Earth and the Sun.
- **Gardening Impact:** The gravitational pull is strong, and there is an increase in moisture in the soil, making it an ideal time for

planting seeds and transplanting seedlings. Plants focus on root growth during this phase.

- **Best Activities:** Planting root vegetables (e.g., carrots, potatoes), transplanting, soil preparation.

Waxing Crescent

- **Characteristics:** The Moon starts to become visible, growing from a sliver to a half-moon.
- **Gardening Impact:** Moisture levels are still high, and plants begin to focus on leaf growth. This is a good time for planting leafy greens and above-ground crops.
- **Best Activities:** Planting leafy greens (e.g., lettuce, spinach), herbs, and annual flowers.

First Quarter

- **Characteristics:** The Moon is half-illuminated and continues to grow.
- **Gardening Impact:** Plant energy is directed towards leaf development and vigorous growth. The first quarter is excellent for planting crops that produce seeds outside the fruit.
- **Best Activities:** Planting grains (e.g., corn, wheat), legumes (e.g., beans, peas), and herbs.

Waxing Gibbous

- **Characteristics:** The Moon is more than half but not fully illuminated.

- **Gardening Impact:** Plants continue to focus on foliage and stem growth, preparing for flowering and fruiting. This phase is ideal for transplanting and grafting.
- **Best Activities:** Transplanting, grafting, fertilizing, pruning to promote growth.

Full Moon

- **Characteristics:** The Moon is fully illuminated, reflecting maximum light.
- **Gardening Impact:** The gravitational pull is strong again, drawing water up into plants. This phase is ideal for harvesting, as plants are rich in moisture and nutrients.
- **Best Activities:** Harvesting fruits and vegetables, planting root crops, watering, and fertilizing.

Waning Gibbous

- **Characteristics:** The Moon starts to decrease in illumination, moving towards the last quarter.
- **Gardening Impact:** Plant energy shifts towards root growth and storage. This is a good time for planting bulbs and perennials.
- **Best Activities:** Planting bulbs (e.g., tulips, daffodils), perennials, and root crops.

Last Quarter

- **Characteristics:** The Moon is half-illuminated and continues to wane.
- **Gardening Impact:** The focus is on root development, and plants' energy is directed downwards. This phase is suitable for pruning and weeding to discourage growth.

- **Best Activities:** Pruning, weeding, harvesting root crops, composting.

Waning Crescent

- **Characteristics:** The Moon is a sliver, approaching the new moon phase.
- **Gardening Impact:** This is a period of rest and preparation for the next cycle. It's a good time for soil amendment and general garden maintenance.
- **Best Activities:** Soil preparation, composting, weeding, planning for the next cycle.

Practical Tips for Gardening by the Moon

To harness the Moon's influence in gardening, follow these practical tips for planting, watering, and harvesting according to lunar phases.

Planting

- **New Moon to Waxing Moon:** Focus on planting above-ground crops, leafy greens, and herbs. The increasing light encourages vigorous growth.
- **Full Moon to Waning Moon:** Plant root crops, bulbs, and perennials. The decreasing light supports root development.

Watering

- **Waxing Moon:** Increase watering as plants are actively growing and need more moisture.
- **Waning Moon:** Reduce watering slightly to prevent waterlogging, as plant growth slows and water uptake decreases.

Harvesting

- **Full Moon:** Harvest fruits, vegetables, and herbs when they are at their peak in moisture and nutrient content.
- **Waning Moon:** Harvest root crops and bulbs, as they will store better and have improved flavor.

Aligning Gardening Activities with Lunar Cycles

Aligning gardening activities with lunar cycles involves more than just following a calendar. It requires observation, intuition, and adaptation to specific garden conditions. Here are some additional strategies to integrate lunar gardening into your practices:

Observation and Adaptation

- **Observe Plant Responses:** Keep a gardening journal to track how plants respond to different lunar phases. Note growth patterns, pest occurrences, and overall health.
- **Adapt to Local Conditions:** Consider local climate and environmental factors. Adjust lunar gardening practices to suit your garden's unique conditions.

Integration with Other Gardening Practices

- **Combine with Biodynamic Gardening:** Integrate lunar gardening with biodynamic practices, which also consider cosmic rhythms and soil health.
- **Use Organic Methods:** Employ organic gardening methods to enhance soil fertility and plant resilience, complementing the natural rhythms of lunar gardening.

Conclusion

Understanding the Moon's role as the Emotional Influencer in gardening allows gardeners to harness its cycles for optimal plant growth and productivity. By aligning planting, watering, and harvesting activities with lunar phases, gardeners can create a more harmonious and successful garden.

Embrace the Moon's influence in your gardening endeavors, and let its cycles guide you in creating a garden that thrives in harmony with the natural rhythms of the cosmos. With careful observation and adaptation, you can cultivate a garden that benefits from the nurturing and transformative power of the Moon.

Chapter 15: Mercury: The Communicator
Influence of Mercury on Gardening

Mercury, the smallest and closest planet to the Sun, is known as the "Communicator" in astrology. Ruled by the element of air, Mercury governs communication, intellect, and agility. Its swift orbit around the Sun influences rapid changes and quick adaptations, making it an essential force in gardening, especially for plants that require fast growth and quick turnaround.

Key Functions of Mercury in Gardening:

- **Communication:** Facilitates the transfer of nutrients and information within plants, enhancing growth and resilience.
- **Intellect and Strategy:** Encourages strategic planning and quick decision-making in gardening practices.
- **Adaptability:** Promotes the growth of quick-growing plants and herbs that thrive on swift cycles.

Best Times for Planting Herbs and Quick-Growing Plants

Herbs and quick-growing plants are highly influenced by Mercury's energy due to their need for rapid growth and frequent harvesting. Understanding the best times to plant and care for these plants can optimize their health and productivity.

Optimal Planting Times for Herbs

Herbs thrive when planted during Mercury's favorable periods, which align with its fast and dynamic energy.

- **Spring Planting:** Early spring is an ideal time for planting most herbs. The soil is warming up, and the days are getting longer, providing the necessary conditions for rapid growth.
  - **Lunar Phase:** Waxing Crescent (to promote lush foliage)
  - **Examples:** Basil, cilantro, parsley, dill

- **Fall Planting:** Some herbs can also be planted in the early fall when temperatures begin to cool but the soil is still warm enough to support growth.
  - ○ **Lunar Phase:** First Quarter Moon (to encourage robust growth)
  - ○ **Examples:** Sage, rosemary, thyme, chives

Optimal Planting Times for Quick-Growing Plants

Quick-growing plants, like leafy greens and certain vegetables, also benefit from Mercury's influence.

- **Early Spring Planting:** Start quick-growing plants as soon as the danger of frost has passed.
  - ○ **Lunar Phase:** Waxing Crescent (to encourage vigorous growth)
  - ○ **Examples:** Lettuce, radishes, arugula, spinach
- **Succession Planting:** Throughout the growing season, especially in early summer, you can continue planting quick-growing crops in succession to ensure a continuous harvest.
  - ○ **Lunar Phase:** Waxing Crescent to First Quarter (for strong initial growth)
  - ○ **Examples:** Baby carrots, green onions, bush beans

Best Gardening Practices Under Mercury's Influence

Gardening under the influence of Mercury requires adaptability, strategic planning, and a focus on plants that benefit from rapid growth cycles. Here are some practices to optimize your gardening efforts under Mercury's guidance:

Planning and Preparation

- **Strategic Garden Layout:** Design your garden to maximize space and efficiency for quick-growing plants and herbs. Consider raised beds and container gardening to optimize soil conditions and ease of access.

- **Soil Preparation:** Ensure soil is well-drained and rich in organic matter. Mercury's influence favors soil that can support rapid nutrient uptake and quick growth.

Planting

- **Seed Starting:** Begin herbs and quick-growing plants from seeds indoors to get a head start on the growing season. Use seed trays and grow lights to simulate optimal conditions.
- **Direct Sowing:** Direct sow seeds of quick-growing plants as soon as the soil can be worked in spring. Thin seedlings to allow enough space for each plant to thrive.

Maintenance

- **Frequent Harvesting:** Regularly harvest herbs and quick-growing plants to encourage continuous growth. Pruning herbs like basil and mint can promote bushier plants and prevent flowering.
- **Nutrient Management:** Apply a balanced, water-soluble fertilizer to support the rapid growth needs of herbs and quick-growing plants. Use compost tea or fish emulsion for an organic boost.

Pest and Disease Control

- **Natural Pest Control:** Utilize companion planting and natural remedies to manage pests. Herbs like basil and marigolds can repel insects, while neem oil and diatomaceous earth can address infestations.
- **Healthy Plant Management:** Maintain plant health by ensuring proper spacing and airflow to prevent fungal diseases. Rotate crops to avoid soil-borne diseases.

Practical Tips for Maximizing Mercury's Influence in the Garden

To fully harness Mercury's energy in your gardening practices, consider the following tips:

Timely Actions

- **Quick Decisions:** Be prepared to make quick decisions regarding planting, watering, and harvesting. Monitor weather conditions and be ready to act swiftly to protect plants from unexpected changes.
- **Succession Planting:** Plan for successive plantings of quick-growing crops to maintain a continuous harvest. This approach aligns with Mercury's dynamic energy and maximizes garden productivity.

Versatility in Plant Choices

- **Diverse Selection:** Grow a diverse array of herbs and quick-growing plants to take advantage of Mercury's influence. Experiment with different varieties to find those that perform best in your garden conditions.
- **Adaptive Practices:** Be flexible in your gardening methods. Adjust planting techniques, watering schedules, and pest management strategies as needed to respond to changing conditions.

Communication and Learning

- **Garden Journal:** Keep a detailed garden journal to track planting dates, growth progress, and harvest yields. Note how plants respond to different phases of the Moon and other astrological influences.

- **Networking:** Connect with other gardeners to share experiences and learn from their successes and challenges. Participate in local gardening groups or online forums to exchange tips and advice.

Conclusion

Mercury, as the Communicator, plays a vital role in gardening by promoting quick growth, adaptability, and strategic planning. By aligning your gardening activities with Mercury's influence, especially when planting herbs and quick-growing plants, you can create a dynamic and productive garden.

Embrace the swift and versatile energy of Mercury in your gardening practices, and let its influence guide you in cultivating a garden that thrives on rapid growth and efficient management. With thoughtful planning and a willingness to adapt, you can maximize the benefits of Mercury's influence and enjoy a bountiful and diverse harvest.

Chapter 16: Venus: The Beautifier
Influence of Venus on Gardening

Venus, the planet of love, beauty, and harmony, is known as the "Beautifier" in astrology. Ruled by the elements of air and earth, Venus governs aesthetics, pleasure, and the appreciation of art and nature. Its influence on gardening is profound, guiding the creation of beautiful, harmonious, and sensory-rich garden spaces. Venus encourages gardeners to focus on visual appeal, fragrance, and the overall sensory experience of their gardens.

Key Functions of Venus in Gardening:

- **Aesthetics:** Promotes the cultivation of visually stunning plants and garden designs.
- **Fragrance and Sensory Experience:** Encourages the inclusion of fragrant and sensory-stimulating plants.
- **Harmony and Balance:** Guides the creation of harmonious and balanced garden spaces.

Best Times for Planting Flowers and Aesthetically Pleasing Plants

Venus' influence is strongest during certain times, making these periods ideal for planting flowers and aesthetically pleasing plants. Understanding these optimal times helps gardeners create the most beautiful and harmonious gardens.

Optimal Planting Times for Flowers

Flowers, with their vibrant colors and pleasing fragrances, are closely associated with Venus. The best times to plant flowers align with Venus' cycles and the Moon's phases.

- **Spring Planting:** Early to mid-spring is an excellent time for planting most flowers. The warming soil and increasing daylight provide optimal conditions for growth.
    - **Lunar Phase:** Waxing Crescent to First Quarter (to promote strong growth and blooming)
    - **Examples:** Tulips, daffodils, hyacinths, pansies
- **Fall Planting:** Late summer to early fall is also a good time for planting certain flowers, particularly bulbs that will bloom in the spring.
    - **Lunar Phase:** Waxing Crescent to First Quarter (to encourage root development)
    - **Examples:** Daffodil bulbs, crocus, chrysanthemums, asters

Optimal Planting Times for Aesthetically Pleasing Plants

Aesthetically pleasing plants, such as ornamental grasses, shrubs, and ground covers, benefit from Venus' influence.

- **Early Spring Planting:** Plant aesthetically pleasing perennials and shrubs in early spring for optimal establishment.
    - **Lunar Phase:** Waxing Crescent (to promote vigorous growth)
    - **Examples:** Lavender, roses, hostas, boxwood
- **Late Summer to Early Fall Planting:** Planting during this period allows plants to establish roots before winter.
    - **Lunar Phase:** First Quarter to Waxing Gibbous (to support root establishment)
    - **Examples:** Ornamental grasses, hydrangeas, coneflowers, sedum

Best Gardening Practices Under Venus' Influence

Gardening under the influence of Venus requires a focus on aesthetics, sensory experiences, and creating a harmonious environment. Here are some practices to optimize your gardening efforts under Venus's guidance:

Planning and Preparation

- **Aesthetic Garden Design:** Venus' love for beauty benefits from a well-thought-out garden design. Incorporate a variety of colors, textures, and plant forms to create visual interest.
- **Soil Preparation:** Ensure soil is rich and well-drained to support the growth of flowers and aesthetically pleasing plants. Incorporate compost and organic matter to improve soil structure and fertility.

Planting

- **Companion Planting:** Use companion planting strategies to enhance the beauty and health of your garden. Pair complementary plants to create visually pleasing combinations and support mutual growth.
- **Layering and Grouping:** Plant in layers and groups to create depth and visual interest. Use tall plants as a backdrop, medium-sized plants in the middle, and shorter plants at the front.

Maintenance

- **Regular Deadheading:** Remove spent flowers regularly to encourage continuous blooming and maintain a tidy appearance.
- **Pruning and Shaping:** Prune and shape plants to maintain their form and promote healthy growth. Use Venus' influence to create harmonious and balanced shapes.

Pest and Weed Control

- **Natural Pest Control:** Embrace Venus' appreciation for nature by using natural pest control methods, such as introducing beneficial insects and using organic sprays.
- **Weed Management:** Maintain a weed-free garden by regularly hand-weeding and using mulch to suppress weed growth and improve soil health.

Practical Tips for Maximizing Venus' Influence in the Garden

To fully harness Venus' energy in your gardening practices, consider the following tips:

Focusing on Beauty and Fragrance

- **Select Fragrant Plants:** Choose plants with pleasing scents to create a sensory-rich garden. Examples include roses, lavender, and jasmine.
- **Incorporate Color:** Use a diverse palette of flower colors to create a visually stunning garden. Consider the color wheel and plant flowers that complement each other.

Creating Harmony and Balance

- **Symmetrical Design:** Use symmetry in your garden design to create a sense of balance and harmony. Mirror plantings and pathways can enhance the garden's overall aesthetics.
- **Soft Lighting:** Incorporate soft garden lighting to highlight key features and extend the enjoyment of the garden into the evening.

Enhancing the Sensory Experience

- **Add Water Features:** Incorporate water features, such as fountains or ponds, to add sound and movement, enhancing the sensory experience of the garden.
- **Use Garden Art:** Add sculptures, garden art, or decorative containers to create focal points and enhance the garden's beauty.

Conclusion

Venus, as the Beautifier, plays a vital role in gardening by promoting beauty, harmony, and sensory richness. By aligning your gardening activities with Venus' influence, especially when planting flowers and aesthetically pleasing plants, you can create a garden that is visually stunning and emotionally uplifting.

Embrace the elegant and harmonious energy of Venus in your gardening practices, and let its influence guide you in cultivating a garden that thrives on beauty and sensory delight. With thoughtful planning and a focus on aesthetics, you can maximize the benefits of Venus's influence and enjoy a garden that is a true feast for the senses.

Chapter 17: Mars: The Energizer

Influence of Mars on Gardening

Mars, the planet of energy, action, and drive, is known as the "Energizer" in astrology. Ruled by the element of fire, Mars governs physical strength, courage, and assertiveness. Its influence on gardening is profound, inspiring vigor, resilience, and robust growth. Mars encourages gardeners to focus on planting hardy and strong plants that can withstand adverse conditions and thrive with minimal care.

Key Functions of Mars in Gardening:

- **Energy and Drive:** Promotes vigorous growth and robust health in plants.
- **Resilience and Strength:** Encourages the cultivation of hardy plants that can endure challenging conditions.
- **Action and Assertiveness:** Guides decisive and timely gardening actions, such as planting and pruning.

Best Times for Planting Hardy and Robust Plants

Mars' influence is strongest during certain times, making these periods ideal for planting hardy and robust plants. Understanding these optimal times helps gardeners create a resilient and vigorous garden.

Optimal Planting Times for Hardy and Robust Plants

Hardy and robust plants, such as root vegetables, perennials, and certain shrubs, benefit from Mars' energizing influence.

- **Early Spring Planting:** Early spring is an excellent time for planting hardy and robust plants. The warming soil and increasing daylight provide optimal conditions for strong growth.

- **Lunar Phase:** Waxing Crescent to First Quarter (to promote vigorous growth and resilience)
- **Examples:** Carrots, potatoes, beets, radishes
- **Fall Planting:** Late summer to early fall is also a good time for planting hardy perennials and shrubs, allowing them to establish roots before winter.
  - **Lunar Phase:** Waxing Crescent to First Quarter (to encourage strong root development)
  - **Examples:** Hardy perennials like echinacea, sedum, and ornamental grasses

Best Gardening Practices Under Mars' Influence

Gardening under the influence of Mars requires a focus on energy, resilience, and decisive actions. Here are some practices to optimize your gardening efforts under Mars' guidance:

Planning and Preparation

- **Vigorous Garden Design:** Mars' love for strength benefits from a garden design that includes hardy and robust plants. Incorporate a mix of perennials, shrubs, and root vegetables to create a resilient garden.
- **Soil Preparation:** Ensure soil is well-drained and rich in organic matter to support the growth of hardy plants. Incorporate compost and organic amendments to improve soil structure and fertility.

Planting

- **Deep Planting:** Ensure plants with deep root systems, like root vegetables and hardy perennials, are planted in well-prepared soil to encourage strong root development.

- **Companion Planting:** Use companion planting strategies to enhance the strength and health of your garden. Pair complementary plants to create resilient plant communities.

Maintenance

- **Regular Pruning:** Mars' assertiveness supports regular pruning to promote healthy growth and prevent overcrowding. Prune shrubs and perennials to maintain their shape and vigor.
- **Consistent Watering:** Ensure consistent and deep watering, especially for newly planted hardy plants. Avoid over-watering by monitoring soil moisture levels.

Pest and Weed Control

- **Natural Pest Control:** Embrace Mars' action-oriented approach by using natural pest control methods, such as neem oil, diatomaceous earth, and beneficial insects.
- **Weed Management:** Maintain a weed-free garden by regularly hand-weeding and using mulch to suppress weed growth and improve soil health.

Practical Tips for Maximizing Mars' Influence in the Garden

To fully harness Mars' energy in your gardening practices, consider the following tips:

Focusing on Strength and Resilience

- **Select Hardy Plants:** Choose plants that are known for their hardiness and resilience. Examples include root vegetables, hardy perennials, and robust shrubs.
- **Strengthen Soil Health:** Improve soil health by incorporating organic matter and ensuring good drainage. Healthy soil supports vigorous plant growth and resilience.

Creating a Dynamic Garden

- **Vary Plant Heights and Forms:** Use a mix of plant heights and forms to create a dynamic and visually interesting garden. Include tall, medium, and low-growing plants for a balanced appearance.
- **Incorporate Structures:** Add garden structures like trellises, arbors, and raised beds to support plant growth and create a more dynamic garden space.

Enhancing Garden Action

- **Timely Actions:** Be prepared to take decisive actions in the garden, such as planting, pruning, and harvesting, to maximize the benefits of Mars' influence.
- **Regular Monitoring:** Monitor the garden regularly for signs of pests, diseases, and stress. Address issues promptly to maintain plant health and vigor.

Conclusion

Mars, as the Energizer, plays a vital role in gardening by promoting energy, resilience, and decisive action. By aligning your gardening activities with Mars' influence, especially when planting hardy and robust plants, you can create a garden that is vigorous and resilient.

Embrace the energetic and assertive energy of Mars in your gardening practices, and let its influence guide you in cultivating a garden that thrives on strength and resilience. With thoughtful planning and a focus on robust plants, you can maximize the benefits of Mars's influence and enjoy a garden that is dynamic, healthy, and vibrant.

Chapter 18: Jupiter: The Expander
Influence of Jupiter on Gardening

Jupiter, the largest planet in our solar system, is known as the "Expander" in astrology. Ruled by the element of fire, Jupiter governs growth, abundance, and prosperity. Its influence on gardening is significant, inspiring expansive growth, bountiful harvests, and the cultivation of fruit-bearing plants. Jupiter encourages gardeners to focus on plants that thrive with space, produce plentiful yields, and contribute to a sense of abundance in the garden.

Key Functions of Jupiter in Gardening:

- **Growth and Expansion:** Promotes vigorous growth and abundant harvests.
- **Prosperity and Abundance:** Encourages the cultivation of fruit-bearing plants and high-yield crops.
- **Optimism and Enthusiasm:** Inspires a positive and expansive approach to gardening.

Best Times for Planting Expansive and Fruit-Bearing Plants

Jupiter's influence is strongest during certain times, making these periods ideal for planting expansive and fruit-bearing plants. Understanding these optimal times helps gardeners create a garden that is bountiful and prosperous.

Optimal Planting Times for Expansive and Fruit-Bearing Plants

Expansive and fruit-bearing plants, such as fruit trees, vines, and high-yield vegetables, benefit from Jupiter's abundant energy.

- **Spring Planting:** Early to mid-spring is an excellent time for planting most expansive and fruit-bearing plants. The warming soil and increasing daylight provide optimal conditions for robust growth.
    - **Lunar Phase:** Waxing Crescent to First Quarter (to promote strong growth and fruit development)
    - **Examples:** Apple trees, grapevines, strawberries, tomatoes
- **Fall Planting:** Late summer to early fall is also a good time for planting certain fruit-bearing plants, allowing them to establish roots before winter.
    - **Lunar Phase:** Waxing Crescent to First Quarter (to encourage root establishment and growth)
    - **Examples:** Raspberry canes, blueberry bushes, figs, garlic

Best Gardening Practices Under Jupiter's Influence

Gardening under the influence of Jupiter requires a focus on growth, abundance, and an enthusiastic approach. Here are some practices to optimize your gardening efforts under Jupiter's guidance:

Planning and Preparation

- **Expansive Garden Design:** Jupiter's love for growth benefits from a garden design that includes ample space for expansive plants. Incorporate fruit trees, vines, and high-yield vegetables to create a bountiful garden.
- **Soil Preparation:** Ensure soil is rich and well-drained to support the growth of expansive and fruit-bearing plants. Incorporate compost and organic matter to improve soil fertility and structure.

Planting

- **Wide Spacing:** Ensure plants have ample space to grow and expand. Fruit trees and vines, in particular, require adequate spacing to thrive.
- **Companion Planting:** Use companion planting strategies to enhance the growth and productivity of your garden. Pair complementary plants to create mutually beneficial relationships.

Maintenance

- **Regular Feeding:** Jupiter's abundant energy supports regular feeding of plants. Use a balanced fertilizer to promote healthy growth and abundant fruiting.
- **Pruning and Training:** Use Jupiter's expansive nature to regularly prune and train fruit trees and vines to maximize yields and maintain healthy growth.

Pest and Weed Control

- **Natural Pest Control:** Embrace Jupiter's positive approach by using natural pest control methods, such as introducing beneficial insects and using organic sprays.
- **Weed Management:** Maintain a weed-free garden by regularly hand-weeding and using mulch to suppress weed growth and improve soil health.

Practical Tips for Maximizing Jupiter's Influence in the Garden

To fully harness Jupiter's energy in your gardening practices, consider the following tips:

Focusing on Growth and Abundance

- **Select High-Yield Plants:** Choose plants that are known for their high yields and expansive growth. Examples include fruit trees, vines, and high-yield vegetables.
- **Improve Soil Health:** Enhance soil fertility by incorporating organic matter and ensuring good drainage. Healthy soil supports vigorous plant growth and abundant harvests.

Creating an Abundant Garden

- **Vary Plant Heights and Forms:** Use a mix of plant heights and forms to create a dynamic and visually interesting garden. Include tall, medium, and low-growing plants for a balanced appearance.
- **Incorporate Structures:** Add garden structures like trellises, arbors, and raised beds to support plant growth and create a more dynamic garden space.

Enhancing Garden Enthusiasm

- **Timely Actions:** Be prepared to take decisive actions in the garden, such as planting, pruning, and harvesting, to maximize the benefits of Jupiter's influence.
- **Regular Monitoring:** Monitor the garden regularly for signs of pests, diseases, and stress. Address issues promptly to maintain plant health and vigor.

Examples of Expansive and Fruit-Bearing Plants to Grow Under Jupiter's Influence

To further illustrate the kinds of plants that thrive under Jupiter's expansive energy, consider incorporating the following into your garden:

Fruit Trees

- **Apple Trees:** Known for their abundant fruit production and variety.
- **Pear Trees:** Produces sweet and juicy fruits that are great for fresh eating and preserving.
- **Cherry Trees:** Offers beautiful blossoms in spring and delicious fruits in summer.
- **Plum Trees:** Provides a bountiful harvest of sweet and tart fruits.

Vines and Climbing Plants

- **Grapevines:** Ideal for producing grapes for fresh eating, juicing, or winemaking.
- **Kiwi Vines:** Yields exotic and nutrient-rich fruits.
- **Clematis:** Known for its vigorous growth and stunning flowers.

High-Yield Vegetables

- **Tomatoes:** A staple in many gardens, known for their prolific fruiting.
- **Zucchini:** Provides abundant harvests and requires minimal care.
- **Peppers:** Offers a variety of colors, flavors, and heat levels.

Conclusion

Jupiter, as the Expander, plays a vital role in gardening by promoting growth, abundance, and a positive approach. By aligning your gardening activities with Jupiter's influence, especially when planting expansive and fruit-bearing plants, you can create a garden that is bountiful and prosperous.

Embrace the enthusiastic and abundant energy of Jupiter in your gardening practices, and let its influence guide you in cultivating a garden that thrives on growth and prosperity. With thoughtful planning and a focus on high-yield plants, you can maximize the benefits of Jupiter's influence and enjoy a garden that is dynamic, healthy, and over-flowing with harvests.

Chapter 19: Saturn: The Disciplinarian
Influence of Saturn on Gardening

Saturn, known as the "Disciplinarian" in astrology, is the planet of structure, discipline, and long-term goals. Ruled by the element of earth, Saturn governs perseverance, patience, and resilience. Its influence on gardening is significant, inspiring a methodical approach, careful planning, and the cultivation of long-term and slow-growing plants. Saturn encourages gardeners to focus on plants that require patience and dedication, ultimately yielding rewarding results over time.

Key Functions of Saturn in Gardening:

- **Structure and Discipline:** Promotes methodical planning and disciplined maintenance in gardening.
- **Patience and Perseverance:** Encourages the cultivation of plants that require long-term care and attention.
- **Resilience and Longevity:** Supports the growth of resilient plants that thrive over extended periods.

Best Times for Planting Long-Term and Slow-Growing Plants

Saturn's influence is strongest during certain times, making these periods ideal for planting long-term and slow-growing plants. Understanding these optimal times helps gardeners create a garden that is resilient and enduring.

Optimal Planting Times for Long-Term and Slow-Growing Plants

Long-term and slow-growing plants, such as perennials, trees, and shrubs, benefit from Saturn's disciplined energy.

- **Early Spring Planting:** Early to mid-spring is an excellent time for planting long-term and slow-growing plants. The soil is warming up, and the days are getting longer, providing optimal conditions for root establishment.

- **Lunar Phase:** Waning Crescent to New Moon (to promote strong root development)
- **Examples:** Oak trees, pine trees, lavender, rosemary
- **Fall Planting:** Late summer to early fall is also a good time for planting certain long-term plants, allowing them to establish roots before winter.
  - **Lunar Phase:** Waning Crescent to New Moon (to encourage root establishment and growth)
  - **Examples:** Fruit trees like apple and pear, evergreen shrubs, perennial herbs

Best Gardening Practices Under Saturn's Influence

Gardening under the influence of Saturn requires a focus on structure, patience, and resilience. Here are some practices to optimize your gardening efforts under Saturn's guidance:

Planning and Preparation

- **Structured Garden Design:** Saturn's love for structure benefits from a well-organized garden design. Incorporate clear pathways, raised beds, and well-defined planting areas to create an orderly garden.
- **Soil Preparation:** Ensure soil is well-drained and enriched with organic matter to support the growth of long-term and slow-growing plants. Regularly amend the soil to maintain fertility and structure.

Planting

- **Deep Planting:** Ensure plants with deep root systems, like trees and shrubs, are planted in well-prepared soil to encourage strong root development.

- **Companion Planting:** Use companion planting strategies to enhance the health and resilience of your garden. Pair complementary plants to create supportive plant communities.

Maintenance

- **Consistent Care:** Saturn's disciplined nature supports regular and consistent care. Water plants deeply and regularly, especially during dry spells, and monitor for signs of pests and diseases.
- **Pruning and Training:** Use Saturn's methodical approach to regularly prune and train trees and shrubs to maintain their shape and promote healthy growth.

Pest and Weed Control

- **Natural Pest Control:** Embrace Saturn's disciplined approach by using natural pest control methods, such as neem oil, diatomaceous earth, and beneficial insects.
- **Weed Management:** Maintain a weed-free garden by regularly hand-weeding and using mulch to suppress weed growth and improve soil health.

Practical Tips for Maximizing Saturn's Influence in the Garden

To fully harness Saturn's energy in your gardening practices, consider the following tips:

Focusing on Structure and Longevity

- **Select Long-Term Plants:** Choose plants that are known for their longevity and resilience. Examples include perennials, trees, and shrubs.

- **Strengthen Soil Health:** Improve soil health by incorporating organic matter and ensuring good drainage. Healthy soil supports long-term plant growth and resilience.

Creating a Structured Garden

- **Clear Pathways and Borders:** Use clear pathways and well-defined borders to create a structured and orderly garden. This helps in maintaining an organized space.
- **Incorporate Permanent Structures:** Add permanent garden structures like raised beds, trellises, and stone pathways to enhance the garden's structure and longevity.

Enhancing Garden Patience

- **Timely Actions:** Be prepared to take timely actions in the garden, such as planting, pruning, and harvesting, to maximize the benefits of Saturn's influence.
- **Regular Monitoring:** Monitor the garden regularly for signs of pests, diseases, and stress. Address issues promptly to maintain plant health and vigor.

Examples of Long-Term and Slow-Growing Plants to Grow Under Saturn's Influence

To further illustrate the kinds of plants that thrive under Saturn's disciplined energy, consider incorporating the following into your garden:

Trees and Shrubs

- **Oak Trees:** Known for their longevity and strength, providing shade and habitat for wildlife.
- **Pine Trees:** Evergreen trees that offer year-round greenery and are highly resilient.

- **Apple and Pear Trees:** Fruit trees that require patience but provide bountiful harvests over time.

Perennials

- **Lavender:** A hardy perennial herb known for its fragrance and medicinal properties.
- **Rosemary:** A resilient herb that can live for many years and offers culinary and medicinal benefits.
- **Echinacea:** A perennial flower known for its health benefits and attracting pollinators.

Evergreen Shrubs

- **Boxwood:** Provides structure and greenery year-round, often used for hedging.
- **Holly:** Offers vibrant berries and glossy leaves, adding winter interest.
- **Juniper:** A hardy shrub that thrives in various conditions and provides year-round interest.

Conclusion

Saturn, as the Disciplinarian, plays a vital role in gardening by promoting structure, discipline, and long-term growth. By aligning your gardening activities with Saturn's influence, especially when planting long-term and slow-growing plants, you can create a garden that is resilient and enduring.

Embrace the disciplined and resilient energy of Saturn in your gardening practices, and let its influence guide you in cultivating a garden that thrives on structure and patience. With thoughtful planning and a focus on long-term plants, you can maximize the benefits of Saturn's influence and enjoy a garden that is robust, healthy, and enduring.

Chapter 20: Uranus: The Innovator
Influence of Uranus on Gardening

Uranus, known as the "Innovator" in astrology, is the planet of change, originality, and revolution. Ruled by the element of air, Uranus governs innovation, experimentation, and the breaking of traditional boundaries. Its influence on gardening is profound, inspiring gardeners to explore new techniques, adopt unconventional practices, and cultivate unusual plants. Uranus encourages a forward-thinking approach, embracing change and creativity to enhance gardening success.

Key Functions of Uranus in Gardening:

- **Innovation and Experimentation:** Promotes the adoption of new gardening techniques and the cultivation of unique plants.
- **Creativity and Originality:** Encourages creative solutions and unconventional garden designs.
- **Adaptability and Change:** Supports the ability to adapt to new conditions and embrace change in the garden.

Best Times for Experimenting with New Gardening Techniques and Unusual Plants

Uranus' influence is strongest during certain times, making these periods ideal for experimenting with new gardening techniques and unusual plants. Understanding these optimal times helps gardeners create a dynamic and innovative garden.

Optimal Times for Experimenting with New Gardening Techniques

Experimenting with new gardening techniques, such as hydroponics, vertical gardening, or permaculture, benefits from Uranus' innovative energy.

- **Spring and Early Summer:** Early to mid-spring is an excellent time to start experimenting with new gardening techniques. The growing season is just beginning, providing ample time to test and refine new methods.
  - **Lunar Phase:** Waxing Crescent to First Quarter (to promote growth and adaptation)
  - **Examples:** Setting up hydroponic systems, building vertical gardens, implementing permaculture principles
- **Late Summer to Early Fall:** Late summer to early fall is also a good time for experimenting with new techniques, as the garden is established and conditions are stable.
  - **Lunar Phase:** First Quarter to Waxing Gibbous (to encourage growth and innovation)
  - **Examples:** Introducing new irrigation methods, experimenting with companion planting, trialing new pest control techniques

Optimal Times for Planting Unusual Plants

Unusual plants, such as rare species, exotic varieties, and unconventional cultivars, thrive under Uranus' influence.

- **Spring Planting:** Early to mid-spring is an ideal time for planting unusual plants, as the soil is warming up and daylight is increasing.
  - **Lunar Phase:** Waxing Crescent to First Quarter (to promote strong growth and establishment)
  - **Examples:** Exotic fruits, rare flowers, heirloom vegetables
- **Fall Planting:** Late summer to early fall is also a good time for planting certain unusual plants, allowing them to establish roots before winter.
  - **Lunar Phase:** Waxing Crescent to First Quarter (to encourage root development)

- **Examples:** Uncommon bulbs, rare shrubs, unique perennials

Best Gardening Practices Under Uranus' Influence

Gardening under the influence of Uranus requires a focus on innovation, creativity, and adaptability. Here are some practices to optimize your gardening efforts under Uranus' guidance:

Planning and Preparation

- **Innovative Garden Design:** Uranus' love for originality benefits from a creative garden design. Incorporate unconventional layouts, unique plant combinations, and innovative structures to create a dynamic garden space.
- **Soil and Environment Preparation:** Ensure the garden environment is adaptable to new techniques. Prepare the soil with compost and organic matter to support the growth of unusual plants.

Planting

- **Diverse Plant Selection:** Ensure a diverse mix of plants that reflect Uranus' innovative spirit. Include exotic fruits, rare flowers, heirloom vegetables, and unique perennials to create a varied and interesting garden.
- **Creative Containers and Structures:** Use creative containers and garden structures to support unusual plants and new gardening techniques. Consider vertical planters, hydroponic systems, and unconventional pots.

Maintenance

- **Flexible Care Practices:** Uranus' adaptability supports flexible care practices. Adjust watering schedules, fertilization, and pruning methods as needed to accommodate new techniques and plant varieties.

- **Regular Monitoring:** Use Uranus' innovative energy to regularly monitor plant health and garden conditions. Make timely adjustments to optimize growth and productivity.

Pest and Weed Control

- **Natural and Innovative Pest Control:** Embrace Uranus' forward-thinking approach by using natural and innovative pest control methods, such as introducing beneficial insects, using organic sprays, and trialing new pest deterrent techniques.
- **Weed Management:** Maintain a weed-free garden by regularly hand-weeding and using mulch to suppress weed growth and improve soil health.

Practical Tips for Maximizing Uranus' Influence in the Garden

To fully harness Uranus' energy in your gardening practices, consider the following tips:

Embracing Innovation and Creativity

- **Experiment with New Techniques:** Try out new gardening methods, such as hydroponics, aquaponics, vertical gardening, and permaculture. Keep detailed records of your experiments to track successes and learn from failures.
- **Cultivate Unusual Plants:** Grow rare and exotic plant varieties to add interest and diversity to your garden. Examples include dragon fruit, blue roses, and heirloom tomatoes.

Adapting to Change

- **Be Open to New Ideas:** Stay informed about the latest gardening trends and innovations. Attend gardening workshops, read gardening blogs, and connect with other innovative gardeners to exchange ideas.
- **Flexible Planning:** Create flexible garden plans that allow for adjustments and experimentation. Be willing to change your approach based on new information and observations.

Enhancing Garden Creativity

- **Incorporate Art and Design:** Use garden art, sculptures, and unique plant arrangements to enhance the garden's visual appeal and reflect your creative vision.
- **Create Themed Gardens:** Design themed garden areas, such as a butterfly garden, a sensory garden, or a medicinal herb garden, to explore different aspects of gardening and attract various wildlife.

Examples of Unusual Plants to Grow Under Uranus' Influence

To further illustrate the kinds of plants that thrive under Uranus' innovative energy, consider incorporating the following into your garden:

Exotic Fruits

- **Dragon Fruit:** A striking and exotic fruit with vibrant pink skin and white or red flesh.
- **Kiwi:** A unique and nutrient-rich fruit that grows on climbing vines.
- **Passion Fruit:** An exotic fruit with a sweet-tart flavor and distinctive aroma.

Rare Flowers

- **Blue Rose:** A rare and beautiful flower that adds a unique touch to the garden.
- **Black Tulip:** A striking and unusual flower with deep, dark petals.
- **Corpse Flower (Amorphophallus titanum):** A rare and fascinating plant known for its large, smelly bloom.

Heirloom Vegetables

- **Heirloom Tomatoes:** Unique and flavorful tomato varieties with diverse colors and shapes.
- **Purple Carrots:** A colorful and nutrient-rich variation of the common carrot.
- **Rainbow Chard:** A vibrant and nutritious leafy green with colorful stems.

Conclusion

Uranus, as the Innovator, plays a vital role in gardening by promoting innovation, creativity, and adaptability. By aligning your gardening activities with Uranus' influence, especially when experimenting with new gardening techniques and unusual plants, you can create a garden that is dynamic and forward-thinking.

Embrace the innovative and creative energy of Uranus in your gardening practices, and let its influence guide you in cultivating a garden that thrives on originality and adaptability. With thoughtful planning and a focus on new techniques and unique plants, you can maximize the benefits of Uranus's influence and enjoy a garden that is both exciting and productive.

Chapter 21: Neptune: The Dreamer
Influence of Neptune on Gardening

Neptune, known as the "Dreamer" in astrology, is the planet of intuition, dreams, and the subconscious. Ruled by the element of water, Neptune governs creativity, spirituality, and a deep connection to the unseen and mystical aspects of life. Its influence on gardening is profound, encouraging gardeners to engage in intuitive practices, embrace water elements, and cultivate plants that thrive in aquatic environments. Neptune inspires a dreamy, meditative approach to gardening, creating serene and mystical garden spaces.

Key Functions of Neptune in Gardening:

- **Intuition and Creativity:** Promotes intuitive gardening practices and creative garden designs.
- **Spiritual Connection:** Encourages a deeper connection to the natural and spiritual aspects of gardening.
- **Aquatic Elements:** Supports the cultivation of aquatic plants and the integration of water features.

Best Times for Planting Aquatic Plants and Engaging in Intuitive Gardening Practices

Neptune's influence is strongest during certain times, making these periods ideal for planting aquatic plants and engaging in intuitive gardening practices. Understanding these optimal times helps gardeners create serene and mystical garden spaces.

Optimal Times for Planting Aquatic Plants

Aquatic plants, such as water lilies, lotus, and other water-loving plants, benefit from Neptune's dreamy and water-infused energy.

- **Late Spring to Early Summer:** Early to mid-spring is an excellent time for planting most aquatic plants. The water temperature is rising, providing optimal conditions for root establishment and growth.

- ○ **Lunar Phase:** Waxing Crescent to First Quarter (to promote strong growth and establishment)
- ○ **Examples:** Water lilies, lotus, water hyacinth, duckweed
- **Early Fall:** Late summer to early fall is also a good time for planting certain aquatic plants, allowing them to establish before the winter months.
  - ○ **Lunar Phase:** Waxing Crescent to First Quarter (to encourage root development and adaptation)
  - ○ **Examples:** Hardy water lilies, marginal plants, water irises

Optimal Times for Engaging in Intuitive Gardening Practices

Intuitive gardening practices, such as meditation in the garden, moon gardening, and planting by feel, thrive under Neptune's influence.

- **New Moon to Full Moon:** The waxing phase of the moon, from New Moon to Full Moon, is a powerful time for engaging in intuitive gardening practices. This phase enhances creativity, intuition, and spiritual connection.
  - ○ **Lunar Phase:** Waxing Crescent to Full Moon (to promote intuitive insights and creative inspiration)
  - ○ **Activities:** Meditation in the garden, moon gardening, intuitive planting
- **Early Morning and Late Evening:** These times of the day, when the world is quiet and the light is soft, are ideal for engaging in intuitive gardening practices. The tranquility and gentle light enhance the connection to the intuitive and spiritual realms.
  - ○ **Times:** Early morning (dawn) and late evening (dusk)
  - ○ **Activities:** Quiet contemplation, meditative gardening, connecting with the garden's energy

Best Gardening Practices Under Neptune's Influence

Gardening under the influence of Neptune requires a focus on intuition, creativity, and a deep connection to water elements. Here are some practices to optimize your gardening efforts under Neptune's guidance:

Planning and Preparation

- **Intuitive Garden Design:** Neptune's love for dreams and intuition benefits from a garden design that incorporates water features, flowing lines, and mystical elements. Create serene spaces with ponds, streams, and waterfalls to enhance the garden's tranquility.
- **Soil and Environment Preparation:** Ensure the garden environment is conducive to intuitive gardening practices. Prepare the soil with organic matter and maintain moisture levels to support the growth of water-loving plants.

Planting

- **Aquatic Plant Selection:** Ensure a diverse mix of aquatic plants that reflect Neptune's water-infused spirit. Include water lilies, lotus, marginal plants, and floating plants to create a varied and interesting water garden.
- **Creative Planting:** Use creative and intuitive planting techniques to enhance the garden's mystical appeal. Consider planting by feel, moon phases, and using symbols or spiritual guidance.

Maintenance

- **Consistent Care:** Neptune's intuitive nature supports regular and consistent care of aquatic plants. Ensure proper water quality, regular feeding, and pruning to maintain the health and beauty of water plants.

- **Natural Maintenance:** Use Neptune's connection to nature to maintain the garden organically. Avoid synthetic chemicals and instead use natural methods for pest control and fertilization.

Pest and Weed Control

- **Natural Pest Control:** Embrace Neptune's intuitive approach by using natural pest control methods, such as introducing beneficial insects, using organic sprays, and planting companion plants that deter pests.
- **Weed Management:** Maintain a weed-free garden by regularly hand-weeding and using natural mulches to suppress weed growth and improve soil health.

Practical Tips for Maximizing Neptune's Influence in the Garden

To fully harness Neptune's energy in your gardening practices, consider the following tips:

Embracing Intuition and Creativity

- **Intuitive Planting:** Plant based on intuition and feel rather than strict schedules. Trust your instincts when choosing plant locations and combinations.
- **Engage in Meditation:** Incorporate meditation into your gardening routine to connect deeply with your garden and enhance your intuitive insights.

Creating a Serene and Mystical Garden

- **Incorporate Water Features:** Use water features like ponds, fountains, and streams to create a serene and mystical garden environment. The sound and movement of water enhance the garden's tranquility.

- **Use Soft Lighting:** Add soft lighting to highlight key features and create a magical ambiance in the garden, especially during early morning and late evening.

Enhancing Spiritual Connection

- **Garden Rituals:** Incorporate garden rituals, such as blessing your plants, moon gardening, and seasonal celebrations, to deepen your connection to the garden.
- **Create Sacred Spaces:** Designate areas of the garden as sacred spaces for meditation, contemplation, and spiritual practices.

Examples of Aquatic Plants and Intuitive Gardening Practices to Grow Under Neptune's Influence

To further illustrate the kinds of plants and practices that thrive under Neptune's dreamy energy, consider incorporating the following into your garden:

Aquatic Plants

- **Water Lilies:** Known for their beautiful and serene blooms, water lilies add elegance and tranquility to any water garden.
- **Lotus:** A symbol of purity and enlightenment, the lotus plant thrives in ponds and water features.
- **Water Hyacinth:** A floating plant with beautiful purple flowers, ideal for adding color to ponds.
- **Duckweed:** A small, floating plant that provides cover for aquatic life and helps maintain water quality.

Intuitive Gardening Practices

- **Moon Gardening:** Plant, water, and harvest according to the lunar phases to align with the natural rhythms of the Moon.

- **Meditative Gardening:** Incorporate meditation and mindfulness practices into your gardening routine to connect deeply with the plants and the garden environment.
- **Symbolic Planting:** Use symbols, such as sacred geometry or spiritual icons, to guide your garden design and planting choices.
- **Seasonal Celebrations:** Celebrate the changing seasons with garden rituals and ceremonies to honor the natural cycles and connect with the garden's energy.

Conclusion

Neptune, as the Dreamer, plays a vital role in gardening by promoting intuition, creativity, and a deep connection to water elements. By aligning your gardening activities with Neptune's influence, especially when planting aquatic plants and engaging in intuitive gardening practices, you can create a garden that is serene and mystical.

Embrace the intuitive and dreamy energy of Neptune in your gardening practices, and let its influence guide you in cultivating a garden that thrives on tranquility and spiritual connection. With thoughtful planning and a focus on water elements and intuitive practices, you can maximize the benefits of Neptune's influence and enjoy a garden that is both peaceful and enchanting.

Chapter 22: Pluto: The Transformer

Influence of Pluto on Gardening

Pluto, known as the "Transformer" in astrology, is the planet of transformation, regeneration, and rebirth. Ruled by the element of water, Pluto governs the deep, unseen processes that bring profound change and renewal. Its influence on gardening is significant, encouraging gardeners to focus on composting, soil regeneration, and the overall health and transformation of their garden ecosystems. Pluto inspires a deep, transformative approach to gardening, fostering practices that rejuvenate the soil and promote long-term sustainability.

Key Functions of Pluto in Gardening:

- **Transformation and Renewal:** Promotes composting and soil regeneration to rejuvenate garden ecosystems.
- **Depth and Insight:** Encourages a deeper understanding of soil health and nutrient cycles.
- **Sustainability and Rebirth:** Supports sustainable gardening practices that contribute to the long-term health of the garden.

Best Times for Composting and Soil Regeneration

Pluto's influence is strongest during certain times, making these periods ideal for composting and soil regeneration activities. Understanding these optimal times helps gardeners create a garden that is healthy, sustainable, and continually renewed.

Optimal Times for Composting

Composting, the process of decomposing organic matter to create nutrient-rich soil, benefits from Pluto's transformative energy.

- **Fall:** Fall is an excellent time for starting or adding to compost piles. The abundance of fallen leaves, garden waste, and kitchen scraps provides ample material for composting.
    - **Lunar Phase:** Waning Moon (to promote decomposition and transformation)
    - **Activities:** Adding leaves, plant debris, and kitchen scraps to compost piles; turning compost to aerate and accelerate decomposition.
- **Spring:** Early to mid-spring is also a good time for composting, as the warming temperatures accelerate the decomposition process.
    - **Lunar Phase:** Waning Moon (to encourage decomposition and nutrient cycling)
    - **Activities:** Starting new compost piles, turning existing compost, and using finished compost to enrich garden soil.

Optimal Times for Soil Regeneration

Soil regeneration, the process of restoring soil health and fertility, thrives under Pluto's regenerative influence.

- **Early Spring:** Early spring is an ideal time for soil regeneration activities, as the soil is beginning to warm up and become active.
    - **Lunar Phase:** Waning Moon (to promote nutrient incorporation and soil health)
    - **Activities:** Adding compost and organic matter to garden beds, practicing crop rotation, planting cover crops.
- **Late Fall:** Late fall, after the main growing season, is also a good time for soil regeneration. This allows the soil to rest and rebuild during the winter months.
    - **Lunar Phase:** Waning Moon (to encourage soil renewal and preparation for the next growing season)
    - **Activities:** Applying mulch, planting cover crops, adding compost and organic amendments.

Best Gardening Practices Under Pluto's Influence

Gardening under the influence of Pluto requires a focus on transformation, regeneration, and sustainable practices. Here are some practices to optimize your gardening efforts under Pluto's guidance:

Planning and Preparation

- **Comprehensive Garden Design:** Pluto's love for transformation benefits from a garden design that incorporates areas for composting, mulching, and soil regeneration. Plan for crop rotation and cover cropping to maintain soil health.
- **Soil Testing:** Conduct regular soil tests to understand the nutrient composition and health of your soil. Use this information to tailor your soil regeneration practices.

Composting

- **Diverse Compost Materials:** Use a diverse mix of compost materials, including kitchen scraps, garden waste, leaves, grass clippings, and manure. This diversity ensures a rich and balanced compost.
- **Aeration and Moisture:** Turn compost piles regularly to aerate and accelerate decomposition. Maintain the right moisture level to support microbial activity and decomposition.

Soil Regeneration

- **Adding Organic Matter:** Regularly add compost, manure, and other organic matter to garden beds to improve soil structure, fertility, and microbial health.

- **Crop Rotation:** Practice crop rotation to prevent nutrient depletion and reduce the risk of soil-borne diseases. Rotate crops based on their nutrient needs and growth habits.

Cover Cropping

- **Planting Cover Crops:** Use cover crops, such as clover, vetch, and rye, to protect and enrich the soil. Cover crops prevent erosion, improve soil structure, and add organic matter.
- **Green Manure:** Incorporate cover crops into the soil as green manure to add nutrients and improve soil health.

Mulching

- **Applying Mulch:** Use organic mulch, such as straw, wood chips, or leaves, to cover the soil surface. Mulch helps retain moisture, suppress weeds, and add organic matter as it decomposes.
- **Maintaining Mulch Layers:** Regularly replenish mulch layers to ensure continuous protection and enrichment of the soil.

Practical Tips for Maximizing Pluto's Influence in the Garden

To fully harness Pluto's energy in your gardening practices, consider the following tips:

Embracing Transformation and Renewal

- **Compost Year-Round:** Keep a compost pile active year-round to continuously recycle organic matter and produce nutrient-rich compost for the garden.
- **Incorporate Diverse Organic Matter:** Use a variety of organic materials in composting and soil regeneration to create a balanced and nutrient-rich environment.

Creating a Sustainable Garden

- **Implement Crop Rotation:** Rotate crops annually to maintain soil fertility and reduce the risk of pests and diseases. Plan your garden layout to facilitate easy rotation.
- **Use Cover Crops:** Plant cover crops during the off-season to protect and enrich the soil. Select cover crops based on their benefits, such as nitrogen fixation or erosion control.

Enhancing Soil Health

- **Regular Soil Testing:** Conduct soil tests every few years to monitor soil health and adjust your soil regeneration practices accordingly.
- **Natural Fertilizers:** Use natural fertilizers, such as compost tea, fish emulsion, and worm castings, to nourish plants and improve soil health.

Examples of Composting and Soil Regeneration Practices to Grow Under Pluto's Influence

To further illustrate the kinds of practices that thrive under Pluto's transformative energy, consider incorporating the following into your garden:

Composting

- **Hot Composting:** A method that accelerates decomposition by maintaining high temperatures in the compost pile. Turn the pile frequently to keep it aerated and active.
- **Vermicomposting:** Using worms to break down organic matter into nutrient-rich castings. Ideal for small spaces and producing high-quality compost.
- **Sheet Composting:** Spreading organic materials directly onto garden beds and allowing them to decompose in place. A simple method for enriching soil without a compost bin.

Soil Regeneration

- **Adding Biochar:** Incorporating biochar into the soil to improve its structure, water retention, and nutrient-holding capacity. Biochar also supports beneficial microbial activity.
- **No-Till Gardening:** Avoiding soil disturbance to preserve soil structure and microbial communities. Use mulch and cover crops to maintain soil health.
- **Mycorrhizal Inoculation:** Adding mycorrhizal fungi to the soil to enhance nutrient uptake and plant health. Mycorrhizae form symbiotic relationships with plant roots.

Conclusion

Pluto, as the Transformer, plays a vital role in gardening by promoting transformation, regeneration, and sustainability. By aligning your gardening activities with Pluto's influence, especially when composting and engaging in soil regeneration, you can create a garden that is healthy, sustainable, and continually renewed.

Embrace the transformative and regenerative energy of Pluto in your gardening practices, and let its influence guide you in cultivating a garden that thrives on renewal and sustainability. With thoughtful planning and a focus on composting and soil health, you can maximize the benefits of Pluto's influence and enjoy a garden that is both vibrant and resilient.

Part 3: Celestial Bodies and Gardening

Chapter 23: Comets and Meteors
Influence of Comets and Meteors on Gardening

Celestial events such as comets and meteors have fascinated humanity for centuries. These cosmic phenomena not only inspire wonder but also have practical implications for gardening and soil composition. Comets and meteors can introduce new elements and minerals to the Earth's surface, impacting soil fertility and plant growth. Understanding their influence allows gardeners to harness these cosmic gifts to enhance their gardens.

Key Functions of Comets and Meteors in Gardening:

- **Soil Enrichment:** Introduces new minerals and elements to the soil, enhancing fertility.
- **Atmospheric Effects:** Influences atmospheric conditions, potentially affecting weather patterns and plant growth.
- **Cultural and Historical Significance:** Inspires traditional and folklore practices in gardening.

Comets and Meteors: An Overview

Comets are icy celestial bodies that originate from the outer regions of the solar system. When they approach the Sun, they heat up and release gases and dust, forming a glowing coma and tail. Meteors, on the other hand, are fragments of comets or asteroids that enter the Earth's atmosphere and burn up, often seen as shooting stars. When meteors survive their journey through the atmosphere and reach the Earth's surface, they are called meteorites.

Composition and Impact:

- **Comets:** Composed of water ice, dust, and organic compounds. When they disintegrate, they can deposit these materials on Earth.
- **Meteors:** Composed of various minerals and metals, including iron, nickel, and silicates. Meteorites enrich the soil with these elements upon impact.

Influence on Soil Composition

Comets and meteors can influence soil composition in several ways. The minerals and elements they introduce can enhance soil fertility, improve plant nutrition, and promote healthy plant growth.

Soil Enrichment:

- **Mineral Addition:** Meteorites can add essential minerals such as iron, magnesium, calcium, and potassium to the soil. These minerals are crucial for plant growth and development.
- **Organic Compounds:** Cometary debris may contain organic compounds that contribute to soil organic matter, improving soil structure and fertility.

Examples of Meteorite Influence:

- **Meteorite Gardens:** Some gardeners incorporate meteorite fragments into their soil or garden designs, believing that the unique minerals and elements can enhance plant growth and vitality.
- **Historical Practices:** Various cultures have used meteorite stones and dust in traditional farming practices, believing in their beneficial effects on crop yields and soil health.

Atmospheric Effects

Comets and meteors can also influence atmospheric conditions, potentially affecting weather patterns and plant growth. While these effects are typically short-lived, they can still have an impact on gardening.

Atmospheric Changes:

- **Meteor Showers:** During meteor showers, the influx of particles can influence atmospheric electricity and ionization, potentially affecting weather patterns.
- **Cometary Dust:** Comets passing close to Earth can release dust that enters the atmosphere, influencing cloud formation and precipitation patterns.

Practical Tips for Harnessing the Influence of Comets and Meteors in Gardening

To harness the potential benefits of comets and meteors in gardening, consider the following practices:

Soil Enrichment with Meteorite Fragments

- **Incorporate Meteorite Fragments:** Add small meteorite fragments to your garden soil. Ensure they are broken down into manageable pieces and evenly distributed to avoid concentrated areas.
- **Meteorite Dust:** Obtain meteorite dust from reputable sources and mix it into your compost or soil to introduce beneficial minerals and elements.

Embrace Traditional Practices

- **Cultural Practices:** Explore traditional gardening practices that incorporate meteorites or cometary influences. Adapt these practices to your gardening approach to enhance soil health and plant growth.

Monitor Atmospheric Conditions

- **Observe Meteor Showers:** Keep track of meteor showers and note any changes in weather patterns or plant behavior during these events. Use this information to adjust your gardening practices as needed.
- **Cometary Events:** Stay informed about upcoming cometary events. Observe how your garden responds and consider incorporating elements of these events into your gardening routine.

Examples of Plants Benefiting from Meteorite-Enriched Soil

Certain plants can particularly benefit from the minerals introduced by meteorites. Consider incorporating these plants into your garden to maximize the benefits:

Leafy Greens

- **Spinach:** Rich in iron, spinach can benefit from the additional iron introduced by meteorite fragments.
- **Kale:** High in calcium, kale can thrive in soil enriched with meteorite-derived calcium.

Root Vegetables

- **Carrots:** Carrots require adequate potassium for root development, which can be enhanced by meteorite minerals.
- **Beets:** Beets benefit from iron and magnesium, both of which can be introduced by meteorites.

Fruit-Bearing Plants

- **Tomatoes:** Tomatoes need calcium to prevent blossom end rot, which can be supplemented by meteorite-enriched soil.
- **Strawberries:** Rich in vitamins and minerals, strawberries can thrive in soil enhanced with meteorite minerals.

Conclusion

Comets and meteors, as celestial phenomena, play a unique role in gardening by influencing soil composition and atmospheric conditions. By understanding their impact and incorporating their benefits into gardening practices, gardeners can enhance soil fertility, promote healthy plant growth, and create a more resilient garden.

Embrace the transformative and enriching energy of comets and meteors in your gardening practices, and let their celestial influence guide you in cultivating a garden that thrives on cosmic gifts. With thoughtful planning and a focus on soil enrichment and atmospheric awareness, you can maximize the benefits of these celestial events and enjoy a garden that is both vibrant and unique.

Chapter 24: Asteroids and Dwarf Planets

Introduction

In addition to the major planets, asteroids and dwarf planets play significant roles in astrological gardening. These celestial bodies, though smaller and less prominent, exert subtle influences that can enhance gardening practices and plant growth. Understanding their roles can provide gardeners with additional tools for cultivating healthy, vibrant gardens.

Understanding Asteroids and Dwarf Planets

Asteroids

Asteroids are small rocky bodies that orbit the Sun, primarily found in the asteroid belt between Mars and Jupiter. They vary in size and composition, often containing valuable minerals and metals.

Dwarf Planets

Dwarf planets are celestial bodies that orbit the Sun and are similar to planets but do not clear their orbital path of other debris. Examples include Pluto, Ceres, and Eris. These bodies have unique characteristics and can influence astrological gardening in distinct ways.

The Role of Asteroids in Astrological Gardening

Asteroids, due to their composition and energy, can subtly influence gardening practices. Here are a few key asteroids and their potential impacts:

Ceres: The Nurturer

Ceres, the largest asteroid in the asteroid belt, is often associated with nurturing, agriculture, and fertility. Its influence can be particularly beneficial for gardeners.

- **Key Functions:** Promotes fertility, enhances soil health, and supports the growth of crops and herbs.

- **Gardening Practices:** Focus on nurturing plants, improving soil fertility, and cultivating crops that require care and attention. Incorporate organic matter and compost to enhance soil health.

Pallas: The Strategist

Pallas is an asteroid associated with wisdom, strategy, and creative problem-solving. Its influence encourages innovative and strategic gardening practices.

- **Key Functions:** Enhances problem-solving, promotes innovative gardening techniques, and supports strategic planning.
- **Gardening Practices:** Experiment with new gardening methods, such as permaculture, companion planting, and integrated pest management. Use strategic planning to optimize garden layout and plant health.

Juno: The Protector

Juno is linked to partnerships, relationships, and protection. In gardening, Juno's influence can help create harmonious and balanced garden environments.

- **Key Functions:** Promotes harmony, supports plant relationships, and enhances protection.
- **Gardening Practices:** Focus on companion planting to create mutually beneficial plant relationships. Use natural pest control methods to protect plants from pests and diseases.

Vesta: The Keeper of the Flame

Vesta is associated with home, hearth, and dedicated service. In gardening, Vesta's influence encourages dedication, focus, and the cultivation of sacred spaces.

- **Key Functions:** Enhances dedication, supports focused gardening efforts, and promotes the creation of sacred garden spaces.
- **Gardening Practices:** Dedicate specific areas of the garden to sacred or meditative spaces. Focus on maintaining and nurturing long-term plantings, such as perennials and shrubs.

The Role of Dwarf Planets in Astrological Gardening

Dwarf planets, with their unique characteristics, also influence gardening practices. Here are a few key dwarf planets and their potential impacts:

Pluto: The Transformer

Pluto, a dwarf planet known for its transformative energy, has a powerful influence on regeneration and rebirth in gardening.

- **Key Functions:** Promotes transformation, supports composting and soil regeneration, and enhances deep renewal.
- **Gardening Practices:** Focus on composting, soil regeneration, and the transformation of garden spaces. Incorporate practices that promote deep renewal, such as adding organic matter and rotating crops.

Ceres: The Nurturer (Revisited)

As both an asteroid and a dwarf planet, Ceres' influence is particularly strong in gardening.

- **Key Functions:** Enhances fertility, promotes nurturing, and supports agricultural practices.
- **Gardening Practices:** Prioritize soil health and fertility, nurture plants through consistent care, and cultivate crops that require attention and dedication.

Eris: The Disruptor

Eris, known for its disruptive energy, can influence gardeners to embrace change and adapt to unexpected challenges.

- **Key Functions:** Promotes adaptability, supports resilience, and encourages embracing change.
- **Gardening Practices:** Be open to experimenting with new plants and gardening methods. Use adaptive techniques to respond to changing conditions and unexpected challenges in the garden.

Practical Tips for Integrating Asteroids and Dwarf Planets into Gardening Practices

To harness the subtle influences of asteroids and dwarf planets in your gardening practices, consider the following tips:

Embrace Nurturing and Fertility

- **Enhance Soil Health:** Focus on improving soil fertility by adding organic matter, compost, and natural fertilizers.
- **Nurture Plants:** Provide consistent care and attention to plants, especially those that require regular maintenance and nurturing.

Experiment with Innovative Techniques

- **Try New Methods:** Experiment with innovative gardening techniques, such as permaculture, hydroponics, and companion planting.
- **Strategic Planning:** Use strategic planning to optimize garden layout, plant placement, and resource management.

Create Harmonious and Sacred Spaces

- **Companion Planting:** Use companion planting to create harmonious plant relationships and enhance garden health.
- **Sacred Spaces:** Dedicate areas of the garden to meditation, reflection, and spiritual practices.

Focus on Transformation and Adaptability

- **Composting and Soil Regeneration:** Prioritize composting and soil regeneration to promote deep renewal and transformation.
- **Embrace Change:** Be open to change and adaptability in your gardening practices. Experiment with new plants and techniques to respond to evolving conditions.

Conclusion

Asteroids and dwarf planets, though less prominent than major planets, play significant roles in astrological gardening. By understanding their influences and incorporating their energies into your gardening practices, you can create a garden that is nurturing, innovative, harmonious, and adaptable.

Embrace the subtle and transformative energy of asteroids and dwarf planets in your gardening practices, and let their influence guide you in cultivating a garden that thrives on fertility, innovation, harmony, and renewal. With thoughtful planning and a focus on soil health, strategic techniques, and sacred spaces, you can maximize the benefits of these celestial bodies and enjoy a garden that is both vibrant and sustainable.

Chapter 25: Constellations and Their Influence

Introduction

Constellations, the groupings of stars forming patterns in the night sky, have been significant in human history, guiding navigation, storytelling, and agricultural practices. In astrological gardening, constellations influence different types of plants and gardening cycles. By understanding these celestial patterns, gardeners can optimize planting, care, and harvesting practices to enhance garden health and productivity.

Understanding the Influence of Constellations

Constellations influence gardening through their association with the zodiac signs and their elemental qualities (fire, earth, air, and water). Each constellation governs specific aspects of plant growth and garden activities. Recognizing these influences helps gardeners align their efforts with celestial cycles, enhancing plant vitality and garden harmony.

The Zodiac Constellations and Their Elements

1. **Fire Signs: Aries, Leo, Sagittarius**
   - **Characteristics:** Promote vigorous growth, flowering, and fruiting. Favor plants that thrive in bright sunlight and warm conditions.
   - **Best Practices:** Focus on planting flowering plants, fruit-bearing trees, and heat-loving vegetables.
2. **Earth Signs: Taurus, Virgo, Capricorn**
   - **Characteristics:** Support root development, stability, and nourishment. Favor plants that require robust root systems and steady growth.
   - **Best Practices:** Focus on planting root vegetables, perennials, and plants requiring rich, fertile soil.

3. **Air Signs: Gemini, Libra, Aquarius**
    ◦ **Characteristics:** Enhance communication, balance, and aerial growth. Favor plants that grow upward or require good air circulation.
    ◦ **Best Practices:** Focus on planting climbing plants, herbs, and flowers that need ample airflow.
4. **Water Signs: Cancer, Scorpio, Pisces**
    ◦ **Characteristics:** Promote moisture, intuition, and sensitivity. Favor plants that thrive in moist environments and require delicate care.
    ◦ **Best Practices:** Focus on planting leafy greens, aquatic plants, and moisture-loving flowers.

Detailed Influence of Each Zodiac Constellation on Gardening
Aries: The Ram (March 21 - April 19)

- **Element:** Fire
- **Characteristics:** Energetic, pioneering, and vigorous.
- **Influence:** Promotes rapid growth and early planting.
- **Best Plants:** Peppers, radishes, marigolds, sunflowers.
- **Gardening Activities:** Start seeds indoors, transplant seedlings, and encourage early blooming.

Taurus: The Bull (April 20 - May 20)

- **Element:** Earth
- **Characteristics:** Stable, patient, and nurturing.
- **Influence:** Enhances root growth and soil fertility.
- **Best Plants:** Root vegetables (carrots, potatoes), roses, spinach.
- **Gardening Activities:** Focus on soil preparation, planting root crops, and mulching.

Gemini: The Twins (May 21 - June 20)

- **Element:** Air
- **Characteristics:** Communicative, versatile, and curious.
- **Influence:** Supports aerial growth and plant communication.
- **Best Plants:** Herbs (basil, dill), climbing plants (beans, peas), ferns.
- **Gardening Activities:** Plant herbs and climbers, ensure good air circulation, and prune for shape.

Cancer: The Crab (June 21 - July 22)

- **Element:** Water
- **Characteristics:** Nurturing, intuitive, and sensitive.
- **Influence:** Promotes moisture retention and leafy growth.
- **Best Plants:** Leafy greens (lettuce, kale), moonflowers, water lilies.
- **Gardening Activities:** Plant leafy greens, ensure consistent watering, and create water features.

Leo: The Lion (July 23 - August 22)

- **Element:** Fire
- **Characteristics:** Bold, creative, and radiant.
- **Influence:** Encourages vibrant blooms and fruiting.
- **Best Plants:** Sunflowers, citrus trees, marigolds, zinnias.
- **Gardening Activities:** Focus on flowering plants, fruit trees, and ensure full sun exposure.

Virgo: The Virgin (August 23 - September 22)

- **Element:** Earth
- **Characteristics:** Practical, meticulous, and health-focused.
- **Influence:** Supports detailed care and plant health.
- **Best Plants:** Medicinal herbs (lavender, sage), wheat, aloe vera.
- **Gardening Activities:** Plant medicinal herbs, maintain garden order, and practice pest control.

Libra: The Scales (September 23 - October 22)

- **Element:** Air
- **Characteristics:** Balanced, aesthetic, and harmonious.
- **Influence:** Promotes symmetry and aesthetic appeal.
- **Best Plants:** Ornamental flowers (roses, hydrangeas), beans, tulips.
- **Gardening Activities:** Focus on garden design, plant aesthetically pleasing flowers, and ensure balanced plant arrangements.

Scorpio: The Scorpion (October 23 - November 21)

- **Element:** Water
- **Characteristics:** Intense, transformative, and passionate.
- **Influence:** Enhances soil regeneration and deep growth.
- **Best Plants:** Nightshades (tomatoes, eggplants), garlic, blackberries.
- **Gardening Activities:** Focus on composting, soil regeneration, and planting transformative plants.

Sagittarius: The Archer (November 22 - December 21)

- **Element:** Fire
- **Characteristics:** Adventurous, expansive, and optimistic.
- **Influence:** Encourages expansive growth and exploration.
- **Best Plants:** Exotic plants (bird of paradise, hibiscus), fruit trees (fig, pomegranate).
- **Gardening Activities:** Experiment with new plants, plant fruit trees, and ensure ample space for growth.

Capricorn: The Goat (December 22 - January 19)

- **Element:** Earth
- **Characteristics:** Disciplined, ambitious, and structured.
- **Influence:** Supports long-term growth and resilience.
- **Best Plants:** Trees (oak, maple), root vegetables (beets, turnips), evergreen shrubs.
- **Gardening Activities:** Plant long-term crops, focus on soil health, and practice regular maintenance.

Aquarius: The Water Bearer (January 20 - February 18)

- **Element:** Air
- **Characteristics:** Innovative, independent, and forward-thinking.
- **Influence:** Promotes experimentation and unconventional methods.
- **Best Plants:** Unusual plants (pitcher plants, Venus flytraps), air plants (Tillandsia), succulents.
- **Gardening Activities:** Experiment with new techniques, plant unusual varieties, and create innovative garden designs.

Pisces: The Fish (February 19 - March 20)

- **Element:** Water
- **Characteristics:** Dreamy, intuitive, and compassionate.
- **Influence:** Enhances moisture and sensitivity in plants.
- **Best Plants:** Aquatic plants (water lilies, lotus), leafy greens (spinach, chard), ivy.
- **Gardening Activities:** Create water features, plant moisture-loving plants, and engage in intuitive gardening practices.

Integrating Constellation Influences into Gardening Cycles

To optimize gardening practices based on constellation influences, consider the following approaches:

Aligning Planting with Constellation Cycles

- **Planting by Moon Phases:** Coordinate planting activities with the Moon's phases and the corresponding constellations. This enhances plant growth and health.
- **Seasonal Adjustments:** Adjust planting schedules to align with the optimal times for each constellation's influence.

Enhancing Garden Design and Layout

- **Thematic Gardens:** Create garden sections based on constellations and their elements. For example, dedicate a section to water signs with moisture-loving plants and water features.
- **Balanced Planting:** Ensure a balanced mix of plants influenced by different constellations to promote overall garden health and diversity.

Practical Tips for Each Constellation's Influence

- **Fire Signs:** Ensure adequate sunlight and warmth. Use reflective surfaces to enhance light exposure.
- **Earth Signs:** Focus on soil health and structure. Regularly add organic matter and practice crop rotation.
- **Air Signs:** Maintain good air circulation. Use vertical gardening techniques to maximize space.
- **Water Signs:** Ensure consistent moisture levels. Incorporate water features and mulch to retain soil moisture.

Conclusion

Constellations, through their association with zodiac signs and elements, play a significant role in astrological gardening. By understanding their influences and integrating their energies into gardening practices, gardeners can enhance plant health, optimize growth cycles, and create harmonious garden spaces.

Embrace the cosmic influence of constellations in your gardening practices, and let their guidance help you cultivate a garden that thrives on celestial rhythms and natural harmony. With thoughtful planning and a focus on constellation-based practices, you can maximize the benefits of these celestial patterns and enjoy a garden that is vibrant, balanced, and bountiful.

Part 4: Moon Phases and Gardening

Chapter 26: New Moon: Planting and Beginnings

Introduction

The New Moon, marking the beginning of the lunar cycle, is a time of new beginnings, growth, and regeneration. In gardening, the New Moon phase is considered ideal for planting seeds, transplanting seedlings, and starting new projects. This phase, when the moon is not visible in the sky, signifies a period of increased moisture in the soil and heightened plant energy, making it an excellent time for initiating new growth.

Understanding the New Moon's Influence on Gardening

The New Moon's influence on gardening is rooted in its gravitational pull and its impact on soil moisture and plant vitality. During this phase, the gravitational forces draw water up towards the soil surface, enhancing soil moisture and seed germination. Additionally, plants tend to focus their energy on root development during the New Moon, establishing a strong foundation for future growth.

Key Benefits of Planting During the New Moon:

- **Enhanced Soil Moisture:** Increased soil moisture aids seed germination and root establishment.
- **Root Development:** Plants focus on developing robust root systems during this phase.
- **Optimal Start:** The New Moon is an ideal time to initiate new planting projects and garden activities.

Best Practices for Planting During the New Moon

To maximize the benefits of planting during the New Moon, gardeners should follow specific best practices that align with this phase's unique characteristics.

Preparing the Garden

1. **Soil Preparation:** Ensure the soil is well-prepared by tilling and adding organic matter such as compost or well-rotted manure. This improves soil structure, fertility, and moisture retention.
2. **Moisture Management:** Water the soil thoroughly before planting to take advantage of the increased soil moisture during the New Moon.

Selecting Suitable Plants

The New Moon phase is particularly favorable for planting seeds, transplanting seedlings, and starting new plants that require strong root development. Here are some suitable plants for this phase:

1. **Leafy Greens:**
   - **Examples:** Lettuce, spinach, kale, arugula.
   - **Benefits:** These plants benefit from the enhanced soil moisture and root development during the New Moon.
2. **Root Vegetables:**
   - **Examples:** Carrots, radishes, beets, turnips.
   - **Benefits:** Root vegetables establish strong root systems during this phase, ensuring healthy growth and abundant yields.
3. **Herbs:**
   - **Examples:** Basil, cilantro, parsley, dill.
   - **Benefits:** Herbs planted during the New Moon tend to develop robust root systems, enhancing their growth and flavor.

4. **Annual Flowers:**
    ◦ **Examples:** Marigolds, zinnias, sunflowers, cosmos.
    ◦ **Benefits:** Annual flowers benefit from the increased energy for root development, leading to strong, vibrant blooms.

Planting Techniques

1. **Direct Sowing:** Sow seeds directly into the prepared soil, following the recommended planting depth and spacing for each type of plant.
2. **Transplanting:** Transplant seedlings into the garden, ensuring they are well-watered and the roots are firmly established in the soil.
3. **Mulching:** Apply a layer of mulch around the base of the plants to retain soil moisture, regulate temperature, and suppress weeds.

Additional Activities

1. **Composting:** Start a new compost pile or add to an existing one. The New Moon's regenerative energy enhances the decomposition process.
2. **Watering:** Ensure consistent and deep watering to support root development. Avoid over-watering to prevent root rot.

Practical Tips for Maximizing New Moon Planting Success

To fully harness the benefits of the New Moon phase in gardening, consider the following practical tips:

Timing and Planning

1. **Lunar Calendar:** Use a lunar calendar to track the New Moon phase and plan your gardening activities accordingly. The New

Moon typically lasts for three days, providing a window for optimal planting.

2. **Weather Conditions:** Monitor weather forecasts and choose a day within the New Moon phase that offers favorable planting conditions, such as mild temperatures and minimal wind.

Enhancing Soil Health

1. **Organic Amendments:** Incorporate organic amendments like compost, aged manure, and green manure crops to enrich the soil and promote healthy root development.
2. **Soil Testing:** Conduct soil tests to determine nutrient levels and pH balance. Adjust soil conditions as needed to provide an optimal growing environment for your plants.

Garden Maintenance

1. **Weeding:** Keep the garden free of weeds, which can compete with newly planted seeds and seedlings for nutrients and water.
2. **Pest Control:** Implement natural pest control methods, such as companion planting, to protect young plants from pests without using harmful chemicals.

Examples of Successful New Moon Planting

To illustrate the effectiveness of New Moon planting, here are some examples of plants that thrive when planted during this phase:

Lettuce

- **Benefits:** Lettuce seeds germinate quickly and develop strong root systems when planted during the New Moon. The increased soil moisture supports rapid growth, resulting in tender and flavorful leaves.

Carrots

- **Benefits:** Carrots planted during the New Moon establish deep and healthy roots, leading to well-formed and sweet-tasting carrots. The initial root development phase is crucial for their overall growth.

Basil

- **Benefits:** Basil seedlings transplanted during the New Moon grow robustly and produce abundant, aromatic leaves. The strong root systems support continuous growth and resilience.

Marigolds

- **Benefits:** Marigold seeds sown during the New Moon germinate quickly and develop strong roots, leading to vibrant and long-lasting blooms. Their presence also helps deter pests in the garden.

Conclusion

The New Moon phase, with its focus on beginnings and root development, offers a unique opportunity for gardeners to initiate new planting projects and enhance plant growth. By following best practices for soil preparation, plant selection, and planting techniques, gardeners can maximize the benefits of this lunar phase and cultivate a thriving garden.

Embrace the regenerative energy of the New Moon in your gardening practices, and let its influence guide you in planting seeds, transplanting seedlings, and starting new projects with confidence. With thoughtful planning and attention to soil health and plant needs, you can create a garden that flourishes under the New Moon's nurturing presence.

Chapter 27: Waxing Crescent: Growth and Expansion

Introduction

The Waxing Crescent phase, occurring just after the New Moon, represents a period of growth and expansion. During this phase, the moon is gradually increasing in illumination, symbolizing a time of building energy and development. For gardeners, this phase is ideal for focusing on activities that promote strong growth and healthy development of plants. Understanding the optimal gardening activities during the Waxing Crescent phase can help maximize plant vitality and garden productivity.

Understanding the Waxing Crescent's Influence on Gardening

The Waxing Crescent phase is characterized by a growing moon that signifies increasing energy and vitality. This phase is associated with upward growth, making it an ideal time for planting above-ground crops, transplanting, and nurturing young plants. The gravitational pull of the moon during this phase encourages the movement of water and nutrients through the soil, supporting robust plant growth.

Key Benefits of Gardening During the Waxing Crescent:

- **Enhanced Growth:** The increasing moonlight supports vigorous growth and development.
- **Upward Energy:** Plants focus on growing leaves, stems, and branches during this phase.
- **Nutrient Uptake:** The movement of water and nutrients through the soil is optimized, promoting healthy plant development.

Optimal Gardening Activities During the Waxing Crescent

To take full advantage of the Waxing Crescent phase, gardeners should engage in specific activities that align with this period of growth and expansion.

Planting Above-Ground Crops

The Waxing Crescent is an excellent time for planting crops that produce their yield above ground. The increasing light and energy support their growth and development.

1. **Leafy Greens:**
    - **Examples:** Lettuce, spinach, kale, Swiss chard.
    - **Benefits:** These plants benefit from the enhanced energy and focus on leaf production.
2. **Herbs:**
    - **Examples:** Basil, parsley, cilantro, dill.
    - **Benefits:** Herbs planted during this phase develop strong stems and lush foliage, enhancing their flavor and aroma.
3. **Flowers:**
    - **Examples:** Marigolds, zinnias, sunflowers, petunias.
    - **Benefits:** Flowering plants thrive during the Waxing Crescent, producing vibrant blooms and healthy growth.
4. **Vegetables:**
    - **Examples:** Tomatoes, peppers, beans, cucumbers.
    - **Benefits:** Vegetables that produce above-ground yields benefit from the increased energy and growth focus.

Transplanting Seedlings

Transplanting seedlings during the Waxing Crescent phase ensures they establish quickly and grow vigorously. The upward energy supports the development of strong stems and leaves.

1. **Preparation:** Ensure the soil is well-prepared with compost or organic matter to provide nutrients for the young plants.
2. **Watering:** Water the seedlings thoroughly before and after transplanting to help them settle into their new environment.
3. **Mulching:** Apply a layer of mulch around the base of the seedlings to retain soil moisture and regulate temperature.

Pruning and Training

Pruning and training plants during the Waxing Crescent phase can promote healthy growth and direct energy towards desired areas.

1. **Pruning:**
    - **Focus:** Remove dead or damaged branches, thin out crowded areas, and shape the plants to encourage balanced growth.
    - **Benefits:** Pruning during this phase helps direct energy towards new growth and enhances plant health.
2. **Training:**
    - **Methods:** Use stakes, trellises, or cages to support plants like tomatoes, beans, and cucumbers.
    - **Benefits:** Training plants during this phase encourages strong, upward growth and prevents damage from sprawling or falling over.

Fertilizing and Feeding

The Waxing Crescent phase is an ideal time to provide plants with the nutrients they need to support vigorous growth.

1. **Organic Fertilizers:** Use organic fertilizers such as compost tea, fish emulsion, or seaweed extract to provide a balanced nutrient supply.
2. **Side-Dressing:** Apply side-dressing of compost or organic fertilizer around the base of established plants to boost their growth.
3. **Foliar Feeding:** Consider foliar feeding, spraying a diluted nutrient solution directly onto the leaves, to provide an immediate nutrient boost.

Pest and Disease Management

Managing pests and diseases during the Waxing Crescent phase can help protect young plants and promote healthy growth.

1. **Natural Remedies:** Use natural pest control methods such as neem oil, insecticidal soap, or introducing beneficial insects like ladybugs and predatory mites.
2. **Healthy Practices:** Maintain good garden hygiene by removing debris, dead leaves, and infected plants to reduce the risk of pests and diseases.

Practical Tips for Maximizing Waxing Crescent Gardening Success

To fully harness the benefits of the Waxing Crescent phase in gardening, consider the following practical tips:

Timing and Planning

1. **Lunar Calendar:** Use a lunar calendar to track the Waxing Crescent phase and plan your gardening activities accordingly. This phase typically lasts for about seven days, providing a window for optimal planting and care.
2. **Weather Conditions:** Monitor weather forecasts and choose a day within the Waxing Crescent phase that offers favorable planting conditions, such as mild temperatures and minimal wind.

Enhancing Soil Health

1. **Organic Amendments:** Incorporate organic amendments like compost, aged manure, and green manure crops to enrich the soil and promote healthy growth.
2. **Soil Testing:** Conduct soil tests to determine nutrient levels and pH balance. Adjust soil conditions as needed to provide an optimal growing environment for your plants.

Garden Maintenance

1. **Weeding:** Keep the garden free of weeds, which can compete with newly planted seeds and seedlings for nutrients and water.
2. **Pest Control:** Implement natural pest control methods, such as companion planting, to protect young plants from pests without using harmful chemicals.

Examples of Successful Waxing Crescent Gardening

To illustrate the effectiveness of Waxing Crescent gardening, here are some examples of plants that thrive when tended to during this phase:

Tomatoes

- **Benefits:** Tomatoes planted or transplanted during the Waxing Crescent phase develop strong stems and vigorous growth, leading to healthy plants and abundant fruit production.

Basil

- **Benefits:** Basil seedlings transplanted during the Waxing Crescent phase grow robustly and produce abundant, aromatic leaves. The strong root systems support continuous growth and resilience.

Marigolds

- **Benefits:** Marigold seeds sown during the Waxing Crescent phase germinate quickly and develop strong roots, leading to vibrant and long-lasting blooms. Their presence also helps deter pests in the garden.

Lettuce

- **Benefits:** Lettuce seeds germinate quickly and develop strong root systems when planted during the Waxing Crescent. The increased soil moisture supports rapid growth, resulting in tender and flavorful leaves.

Conclusion

The Waxing Crescent phase, with its focus on growth and expansion, offers a unique opportunity for gardeners to enhance plant vitality and garden productivity. By following best practices for planting, transplanting, pruning, and feeding, gardeners can maximize the benefits of this lunar phase and cultivate a thriving garden.

Embrace the building energy of the Waxing Crescent in your gardening practices, and let its influence guide you in nurturing plants, promoting growth, and ensuring a bountiful harvest. With thoughtful planning and attention to soil health and plant needs, you can create a garden that flourishes under the Waxing Crescent's expanding presence.

Chapter 28: First Quarter: Strength and Stability

Introduction

The First Quarter phase of the lunar cycle, occurring roughly a week after the New Moon, is a time of significant growth and development. The moon is half-illuminated, symbolizing a period of building strength and establishing stability in the garden. During this phase, plants focus on solidifying their structure, developing robust stems, and expanding their foliage. Understanding the best practices for reinforcing plant growth during the First Quarter can help gardeners ensure their plants are strong and resilient.

Understanding the First Quarter's Influence on Gardening

The First Quarter phase is characterized by increased moonlight and a rising gravitational pull, which supports the upward movement of water and nutrients through the soil. This phase is ideal for activities that enhance plant strength and stability, such as pruning, staking, and fertilizing. Plants are in a phase of active growth, focusing on developing strong stems and expanding their root systems.

Key Benefits of Gardening During the First Quarter:

- **Increased Strength:** The growing moonlight encourages robust stem and root development.
- **Enhanced Stability:** Plants focus on solidifying their structure, making this phase ideal for reinforcing growth.
- **Optimal Nutrient Uptake:** The movement of water and nutrients is optimized, promoting healthy plant development.

Best Practices for Reinforcing Plant Growth During the First Quarter

To maximize the benefits of the First Quarter phase, gardeners should engage in specific activities that align with this period of strength and stability.

Pruning and Training

Pruning and training plants during the First Quarter phase can promote healthy growth and direct energy towards desired areas.

1. **Pruning:**
   - **Focus:** Remove dead or damaged branches, thin out crowded areas, and shape the plants to encourage balanced growth.
   - **Benefits:** Pruning during this phase helps direct energy towards new growth and enhances plant health. It also improves air circulation and light penetration.

2. **Training:**
   - **Methods:** Use stakes, trellises, or cages to support plants like tomatoes, beans, and cucumbers.
   - **Benefits:** Training plants during this phase encourages strong, upward growth and prevents damage from sprawling or falling over.

Staking and Supporting

Providing support to growing plants during the First Quarter phase ensures they develop strong and stable structures.

1. **Staking:**
   - **Materials:** Use stakes made of bamboo, wood, or metal to support tall or top-heavy plants.
   - **Placement:** Insert stakes into the ground close to the plant's base and tie the plant to the stake with soft ties or twine.
   - **Benefits:** Staking helps prevent plants from bending or breaking under their weight, especially during windy conditions.

2. **Trellising:**
    - **Plants:** Suitable for climbing plants like peas, beans, and cucumbers.
    - **Installation:** Set up trellises early in the plant's growth to guide their climbing habits.
    - **Benefits:** Trellising keeps plants off the ground, reducing the risk of disease and promoting better air circulation.

Fertilizing and Feeding

The First Quarter phase is an ideal time to provide plants with the nutrients they need to support vigorous growth and development.

1. **Organic Fertilizers:** Use organic fertilizers such as compost, manure, or fish emulsion to provide a balanced nutrient supply.
2. **Side-Dressing:** Apply side-dressing of compost or organic fertilizer around the base of established plants to boost their growth.
3. **Foliar Feeding:** Consider foliar feeding, spraying a diluted nutrient solution directly onto the leaves, to provide an immediate nutrient boost.

Watering and Moisture Management

Ensuring consistent and adequate watering during the First Quarter phase supports robust plant growth and stability.

1. **Deep Watering:** Water deeply to encourage deep root growth. Ensure the soil is consistently moist but not waterlogged.
2. **Mulching:** Apply a layer of mulch around the base of plants to retain soil moisture, regulate temperature, and suppress weeds.

Pest and Disease Management

Managing pests and diseases during the First Quarter phase can help protect growing plants and promote healthy development.

1. **Natural Remedies:** Use natural pest control methods such as neem oil, insecticidal soap, or introducing beneficial insects like ladybugs and predatory mites.
2. **Healthy Practices:** Maintain good garden hygiene by removing debris, dead leaves, and infected plants to reduce the risk of pests and diseases.

Practical Tips for Maximizing First Quarter Gardening Success

To fully harness the benefits of the First Quarter phase in gardening, consider the following practical tips:

Timing and Planning

1. **Lunar Calendar:** Use a lunar calendar to track the First Quarter phase and plan your gardening activities accordingly. This phase typically lasts for about seven days, providing a window for optimal planting and care.
2. **Weather Conditions:** Monitor weather forecasts and choose a day within the First Quarter phase that offers favorable planting conditions, such as mild temperatures and minimal wind.

Enhancing Soil Health

1. **Organic Amendments:** Incorporate organic amendments like compost, aged manure, and green manure crops to enrich the soil and promote healthy growth.
2. **Soil Testing:** Conduct soil tests to determine nutrient levels and pH balance. Adjust soil conditions as needed to provide an optimal growing environment for your plants.

Garden Maintenance

1. **Weeding:** Keep the garden free of weeds, which can compete with newly planted seeds and seedlings for nutrients and water.
2. **Pest Control:** Implement natural pest control methods, such as companion planting, to protect young plants from pests without using harmful chemicals.

Examples of Successful First Quarter Gardening

To illustrate the effectiveness of First Quarter gardening, here are some examples of plants that thrive when tended to during this phase:

Tomatoes

- **Benefits:** Tomatoes staked and pruned during the First Quarter phase develop strong stems and vigorous growth, leading to healthy plants and abundant fruit production.

Beans

- **Benefits:** Beans supported with trellises during the First Quarter phase grow robustly and produce high yields. The vertical growth reduces disease risk and improves air circulation.

Basil

- **Benefits:** Basil plants pruned and fed during the First Quarter phase produce abundant, aromatic leaves. The strong root systems support continuous growth and resilience.

Zinnias

- **Benefits:** Zinnias staked and fertilized during the First Quarter phase develop sturdy stems and vibrant blooms. Their growth is enhanced by the increasing moonlight.

Conclusion

The First Quarter phase, with its focus on strength and stability, offers a unique opportunity for gardeners to enhance plant vitality and garden productivity. By following best practices for pruning, staking, fertilizing, and supporting plants, gardeners can maximize the benefits of this lunar phase and cultivate a thriving garden.

Embrace the building energy of the First Quarter in your gardening practices, and let its influence guide you in nurturing plants, promoting growth, and ensuring a bountiful harvest. With thoughtful planning and attention to soil health and plant needs, you can create a garden that flourishes under the First Quarter's stabilizing presence.

Chapter 29: Waxing Gibbous: Preparing for Fullness

Introduction

The Waxing Gibbous phase occurs between the First Quarter and Full Moon, marked by the moon being more than half illuminated and continuing to grow in brightness. This phase represents a time of preparation and anticipation, as plants channel energy into developing to their fullest potential. For gardeners, the Waxing Gibbous phase is ideal for activities that support maturation and prepare plants for the peak energy of the Full Moon. Understanding the best practices for gardening during the Waxing Gibbous phase can help ensure a robust and bountiful garden.

Understanding the Waxing Gibbous' Influence on Gardening

The Waxing Gibbous phase is characterized by a high level of lunar energy, fostering vigorous growth and development. This phase encourages plants to focus on flowering, fruiting, and overall maturation. It is a time to enhance the health and resilience of plants, ensuring they are well-prepared for the abundance and energy of the Full Moon.

Key Benefits of Gardening During the Waxing Gibbous:

- **Enhanced Growth:** The increasing moonlight supports vigorous growth and development.
- **Preparation for Fullness:** Plants focus on maturing and preparing for flowering and fruiting.
- **Optimal Nutrient Uptake:** The movement of water and nutrients is optimized, promoting healthy plant development.

Best Practices for Gardening During the Waxing Gibbous

To maximize the benefits of the Waxing Gibbous phase, gardeners should engage in specific activities that align with this period of preparation and growth.

Planting and Transplanting

The Waxing Gibbous phase is still favorable for planting and transplanting activities, particularly for plants that will benefit from the high energy levels leading up to the Full Moon.

1. **Flowering Plants:**
   - **Examples:** Roses, marigolds, petunias, zinnias.
   - **Benefits:** These plants will develop strong blooms and vibrant colors, benefiting from the increasing lunar energy.
2. **Fruit-Bearing Plants:**
   - **Examples:** Tomatoes, peppers, cucumbers, strawberries.
   - **Benefits:** These plants will focus on fruit development, leading to larger and more abundant yields.
3. **Perennials:**
   - **Examples:** Lavender, sage, hostas, daylilies.
   - **Benefits:** Perennials transplanted during this phase will establish strong root systems and prepare for vigorous growth.

Fertilizing and Feeding

Providing nutrients during the Waxing Gibbous phase ensures that plants have the resources they need to support maturation and development.

1. **Organic Fertilizers:** Use organic fertilizers such as compost tea, fish emulsion, or seaweed extract to provide a balanced nutrient supply.

2. **Side-Dressing:** Apply side-dressing of compost or organic fertilizer around the base of established plants to boost their growth.
3. **Foliar Feeding:** Consider foliar feeding, spraying a diluted nutrient solution directly onto the leaves, to provide an immediate nutrient boost.

Pruning and Training

Pruning and training plants during the Waxing Gibbous phase can promote healthy growth and prepare plants for flowering and fruiting.

1. **Pruning:**
   - **Focus:** Remove dead or damaged branches, thin out crowded areas, and shape the plants to encourage balanced growth.
   - **Benefits:** Pruning during this phase helps direct energy towards new growth and enhances plant health. It also improves air circulation and light penetration.
2. **Training:**
   - **Methods:** Use stakes, trellises, or cages to support plants like tomatoes, beans, and cucumbers.
   - **Benefits:** Training plants during this phase encourages strong, upward growth and prevents damage from sprawling or falling over.

Watering and Moisture Management

Ensuring consistent and adequate watering during the Waxing Gibbous phase supports robust plant growth and stability.

1. **Deep Watering:** Water deeply to encourage deep root growth. Ensure the soil is consistently moist but not waterlogged.
2. **Mulching:** Apply a layer of mulch around the base of plants to retain soil moisture, regulate temperature, and suppress weeds.

Pest and Disease Management

Managing pests and diseases during the Waxing Gibbous phase can help protect growing plants and promote healthy development.

1. **Natural Remedies:** Use natural pest control methods such as neem oil, insecticidal soap, or introducing beneficial insects like ladybugs and predatory mites.
2. **Healthy Practices:** Maintain good garden hygiene by removing debris, dead leaves, and infected plants to reduce the risk of pests and diseases.

Practical Tips for Maximizing Waxing Gibbous Gardening Success

To fully harness the benefits of the Waxing Gibbous phase in gardening, consider the following practical tips:

Timing and Planning

1. **Lunar Calendar:** Use a lunar calendar to track the Waxing Gibbous phase and plan your gardening activities accordingly. This phase typically lasts for about seven days, providing a window for optimal planting and care.
2. **Weather Conditions:** Monitor weather forecasts and choose a day within the Waxing Gibbous phase that offers favorable planting conditions, such as mild temperatures and minimal wind.

Enhancing Soil Health

1. **Organic Amendments:** Incorporate organic amendments like compost, aged manure, and green manure crops to enrich the soil and promote healthy growth.
2. **Soil Testing:** Conduct soil tests to determine nutrient levels and pH balance. Adjust soil conditions as needed to provide an optimal growing environment for your plants.

Garden Maintenance

1. **Weeding:** Keep the garden free of weeds, which can compete with newly planted seeds and seedlings for nutrients and water.
2. **Pest Control:** Implement natural pest control methods, such as companion planting, to protect young plants from pests without using harmful chemicals.

Examples of Successful Waxing Gibbous Gardening

To illustrate the effectiveness of Waxing Gibbous gardening, here are some examples of plants that thrive when tended to during this phase:

Tomatoes

- **Benefits:** Tomatoes fertilized and supported during the Waxing Gibbous phase develop strong stems and vigorous growth, leading to healthy plants and abundant fruit production.

Marigolds

- **Benefits:** Marigold seeds sown and fertilized during the Waxing Gibbous phase germinate quickly and develop strong roots, leading to vibrant and long-lasting blooms. Their presence also helps deter pests in the garden.

Cucumbers

- **Benefits:** Cucumbers trained and watered during the Waxing Gibbous phase grow robustly and produce high yields. The vertical growth reduces disease risk and improves air circulation.

Lavender

- **Benefits:** Lavender plants pruned and fed during the Waxing Gibbous phase produce abundant, aromatic flowers. The strong root systems support continuous growth and resilience.

Conclusion

The Waxing Gibbous phase, with its focus on preparing for fullness, offers a unique opportunity for gardeners to enhance plant vitality and garden productivity. By following best practices for planting, transplanting, pruning, and feeding, gardeners can maximize the benefits of this lunar phase and cultivate a thriving garden.

Embrace the building energy of the Waxing Gibbous in your gardening practices, and let its influence guide you in nurturing plants, promoting growth, and ensuring a bountiful harvest. With thoughtful planning and attention to soil health and plant needs, you can create a garden that flourishes under the Waxing Gibbous's expanding presence.

Chapter 30: Full Moon: Harvest and Abundance

Introduction

The Full Moon, the zenith of the lunar cycle, represents a time of culmination, abundance, and heightened energy. During this phase, the moon is fully illuminated, symbolizing completion and fulfillment. For gardeners, the Full Moon phase is ideal for harvesting crops, as plants reach their peak potency and vitality. Understanding the best practices for harvesting during the Full Moon and its impact on plant potency can help ensure a bountiful and high-quality yield.

Understanding the Full Moon's Influence on Gardening

The Full Moon's influence on gardening is profound, marked by increased gravitational pull and maximum moonlight. This phase enhances the movement of water and nutrients within plants, promoting optimal growth and potency. Harvesting during the Full Moon ensures that plants are at their most robust, flavorful, and nutrient-rich state.

Key Benefits of Harvesting During the Full Moon:

- **Peak Potency:** Plants reach their highest concentration of nutrients and flavors during the Full Moon.
- **Increased Water Content:** The heightened gravitational pull increases water content in plants, enhancing their juiciness and vitality.
- **Optimal Growth:** Plants are at their most vigorous and resilient, making it an ideal time for harvesting.

Best Practices for Harvesting During the Full Moon

To maximize the benefits of harvesting during the Full Moon, gardeners should follow specific practices that align with this phase's unique characteristics.

Timing and Preparation

1. **Lunar Calendar:** Use a lunar calendar to track the Full Moon phase and plan your harvesting activities accordingly. The Full Moon typically lasts for three days, providing a window for optimal harvesting.
2. **Weather Conditions:** Monitor weather forecasts and choose a day within the Full Moon phase that offers favorable harvesting conditions, such as dry weather and mild temperatures.

Harvesting Techniques

1. **Harvesting Tools:** Use clean, sharp tools such as pruners, scissors, and knives to ensure precise cuts and minimize damage to plants.
2. **Harvesting Timing:** Harvest plants in the early morning or late afternoon when temperatures are cooler and plants are less stressed.
3. **Handling Crops:** Handle harvested crops gently to avoid bruising and damage. Place them in shaded, cool areas to preserve freshness and quality.

Suitable Crops for Full Moon Harvest

The Full Moon phase is particularly favorable for harvesting a wide range of crops, including fruits, vegetables, herbs, and flowers.

1. **Fruits:**
   - **Examples:** Apples, pears, peaches, berries.

- **Benefits:** Fruits harvested during the Full Moon are juicier and more flavorful, with higher nutrient content.

2. **Vegetables:**
   - **Examples:** Tomatoes, cucumbers, peppers, beans.
   - **Benefits:** Vegetables harvested during the Full Moon are more vibrant, crisp, and nutrient-rich.

3. **Herbs:**
   - **Examples:** Basil, mint, rosemary, thyme.
   - **Benefits:** Herbs harvested during the Full Moon have enhanced aroma, flavor, and medicinal properties.

4. **Flowers:**
   - **Examples:** Roses, sunflowers, marigolds, zinnias.
   - **Benefits:** Flowers harvested during the Full Moon have stronger fragrances, brighter colors, and longer vase life.

Post-Harvest Care

1. **Cleaning:** Clean harvested crops gently to remove dirt and debris without damaging the produce.
2. **Storage:** Store harvested crops appropriately to maintain their freshness and quality. Use cool, dark, and well-ventilated areas for storage.
3. **Preservation:** Consider preserving excess harvest through canning, drying, or freezing to extend its shelf life and enjoy the bounty year-round.

Practical Tips for Maximizing Full Moon Harvesting Success

To fully harness the benefits of the Full Moon phase in gardening, consider the following practical tips:

Enhancing Plant Potency

1. **Optimal Watering:** Water plants adequately in the days leading up to the Full Moon to ensure they are well-hydrated and at their peak potency.
2. **Nutrient Boost:** Apply a final nutrient boost, such as compost tea or diluted fish emulsion, a few days before the Full Moon to enhance plant vitality and nutrient content.

Garden Maintenance

1. **Pest Control:** Implement natural pest control methods to protect crops from pests and diseases in the days leading up to the Full Moon.
2. **Weed Management:** Keep the garden free of weeds to reduce competition for nutrients and water, ensuring that crops reach their full potential.

Examples of Successful Full Moon Harvesting

To illustrate the effectiveness of Full Moon harvesting, here are some examples of crops that thrive when harvested during this phase:

Apples

- **Benefits:** Apples harvested during the Full Moon are juicier, sweeter, and more flavorful. The increased water content enhances their crispness and texture.

Tomatoes

- **Benefits:** Tomatoes harvested during the Full Moon are more vibrant and nutrient-rich. The enhanced flavor and juiciness make them ideal for fresh consumption and preservation.

Basil

- **Benefits:** Basil harvested during the Full Moon has a stronger aroma and flavor, making it perfect for culinary use and herbal preparations.

Roses

- **Benefits:** Roses harvested during the Full Moon have brighter colors and stronger fragrances, making them ideal for bouquets and floral arrangements.

Conclusion

The Full Moon phase, with its focus on harvest and abundance, offers a unique opportunity for gardeners to maximize plant potency and yield. By following best practices for harvesting, timing, and post-harvest care, gardeners can ensure a bountiful and high-quality harvest.

Embrace the peak energy of the Full Moon in your gardening practices, and let its influence guide you in harvesting crops at their most robust and flavorful state. With thoughtful planning and attention to plant needs, you can create a garden that flourishes under the Full Moon's abundant presence, providing a rich and satisfying harvest.

Chapter 31: Waning Gibbous: Reflection and Rest

Introduction

The Waning Gibbous phase follows the Full Moon, marking a period of reflection, rest, and gradual transition. During this phase, the moon's illumination decreases, symbolizing a time for gardeners to review their efforts, consolidate their gains, and prepare for the next lunar cycle. The Waning Gibbous phase is ideal for activities that involve harvesting the remaining crops, performing garden maintenance, and planning future gardening tasks. Understanding the best practices for gardening during the Waning Gibbous phase can help ensure a smooth transition and set the stage for continued success.

Understanding the Waning Gibbous' Influence on Gardening

The Waning Gibbous phase is characterized by a decrease in lunar energy and illumination, which signals a shift from active growth to consolidation and reflection. This phase encourages gardeners to focus on harvesting, soil enrichment, and garden cleanup. It is a time to take stock of what has been accomplished, identify areas for improvement, and prepare the garden for the upcoming cycles.

Key Benefits of Gardening During the Waning Gibbous:

- **Harvest Completion:** Finish harvesting remaining crops to maximize yield and quality.
- **Garden Cleanup:** Remove spent plants, debris, and weeds to prepare the garden for future planting.
- **Soil Enrichment:** Focus on soil health and fertility by adding organic matter and amendments.
- **Planning and Reflection:** Reflect on past gardening practices and plan for future improvements.

Best Practices for Gardening During the Waning Gibbous

To maximize the benefits of the Waning Gibbous phase, gardeners should engage in specific activities that align with this period of reflection and rest.

Harvesting Remaining Crops

The Waning Gibbous phase is ideal for completing the harvest of remaining crops, ensuring that all produce is collected before plants begin to decline.

1. **Vegetables:**
   - **Examples:** Late-season tomatoes, peppers, beans, squash.
   - **Benefits:** Harvesting during this phase ensures that vegetables are collected at their peak quality and prevents spoilage.
2. **Herbs:**
   - **Examples:** Basil, parsley, mint, oregano.
   - **Benefits:** Herbs harvested during the Waning Gibbous phase retain their flavor and aroma, making them ideal for drying or preserving.
3. **Fruits:**
   - **Examples:** Apples, pears, grapes, berries.
   - **Benefits:** Fruits harvested during this phase are ripe and ready for immediate use or preservation.

Garden Cleanup and Maintenance

Cleaning up the garden during the Waning Gibbous phase helps prepare the space for the next planting cycle and prevents the buildup of pests and diseases.

1. **Removing Spent Plants:**
   - **Tasks:** Remove dead or dying plants, along with any remaining fruits or vegetables that are no longer viable.

- **Benefits:** Prevents the spread of pests and diseases and frees up space for future planting.

2. **Weeding:**
   - **Tasks:** Pull weeds and remove any unwanted vegetation to reduce competition for nutrients and water.
   - **Benefits:** Helps maintain soil health and reduces the likelihood of weed problems in the next cycle.

3. **Clearing Debris:**
   - **Tasks:** Collect and dispose of garden debris, such as fallen leaves, twigs, and plant matter.
   - **Benefits:** Reduces the risk of pest infestations and creates a tidy, organized garden space.

Soil Enrichment and Amendment

Focusing on soil health during the Waning Gibbous phase helps prepare the soil for future planting and ensures optimal growing conditions.

1. **Adding Organic Matter:**
   - **Tasks:** Incorporate compost, aged manure, and other organic matter into the soil to improve fertility and structure.
   - **Benefits:** Enhances soil health, promotes microbial activity, and improves water retention.

2. **Mulching:**
   - **Tasks:** Apply a layer of mulch to protect the soil, retain moisture, and suppress weeds.
   - **Benefits:** Helps maintain soil temperature, reduces erosion, and adds organic matter as it decomposes.

3. **Soil Testing and Amendment:**
   - **Tasks:** Conduct soil tests to determine nutrient levels and pH balance. Add amendments as needed to correct deficiencies and create optimal growing conditions.

- **Benefits:** Ensures that the soil is well-prepared for the next planting cycle and supports healthy plant growth.

Planning and Reflection

The Waning Gibbous phase is an ideal time to reflect on past gardening practices, assess successes and challenges, and plan for future improvements.

1. **Garden Journal:**
   - **Tasks:** Record observations, successes, and challenges in a garden journal. Note the performance of different plants, weather conditions, and pest or disease issues.
   - **Benefits:** Provides valuable insights for future gardening practices and helps track progress over time.
2. **Planning Future Planting:**
   - **Tasks:** Plan the next planting cycle, considering crop rotation, companion planting, and garden layout. Select seeds and plants that align with your goals and growing conditions.
   - **Benefits:** Ensures a well-organized and efficient garden plan, maximizing space and resources.
3. **Reviewing and Learning:**
   - **Tasks:** Review gardening resources, such as books, articles, and online forums, to gather new ideas and techniques. Attend gardening workshops or join local gardening groups for additional insights.
   - **Benefits:** Enhances gardening knowledge and skills, leading to improved practices and better results.

Practical Tips for Maximizing Waning Gibbous Gardening Success

To fully harness the benefits of the Waning Gibbous phase in gardening, consider the following practical tips:

Timing and Planning

1. **Lunar Calendar:** Use a lunar calendar to track the Waning Gibbous phase and plan your gardening activities accordingly. This phase typically lasts for about seven days, providing a window for optimal cleanup and preparation.
2. **Weather Conditions:** Monitor weather forecasts and choose a day within the Waning Gibbous phase that offers favorable conditions for outdoor work.

Enhancing Soil Health

1. **Composting:** Start or maintain a compost pile to recycle garden waste and produce nutrient-rich compost for future use.
2. **Cover Crops:** Consider planting cover crops, such as clover or rye, to protect and enrich the soil during the off-season.

Garden Maintenance

1. **Tool Care:** Clean and sharpen gardening tools to ensure they are in good condition for future use.
2. **Infrastructure Maintenance:** Inspect and repair garden infrastructure, such as trellises, fences, and irrigation systems, to ensure they are ready for the next planting cycle.

Examples of Successful Waning Gibbous Gardening

To illustrate the effectiveness of Waning Gibbous gardening, here are some examples of activities that thrive during this phase:

Composting

- **Benefits:** Starting or maintaining a compost pile during the Waning Gibbous phase helps recycle garden waste and produce nutrient-rich compost for future use. The decomposing plant matter adds valuable organic matter to the soil.

Soil Amendment

- **Benefits:** Adding compost and organic matter to the soil during the Waning Gibbous phase improves soil structure, fertility, and water retention. This prepares the soil for the next planting cycle and promotes healthy plant growth.

Garden Planning

- **Benefits:** Reflecting on past gardening practices and planning for the future during the Waning Gibbous phase helps ensure a well-organized and efficient garden layout. This maximizes space and resources and leads to improved gardening outcomes.

Conclusion

The Waning Gibbous phase, with its focus on reflection and rest, offers a unique opportunity for gardeners to consolidate their gains, maintain their garden, and prepare for the next cycle. By following best practices for harvesting, garden cleanup, soil enrichment, and planning, gardeners can ensure a smooth transition and set the stage for continued success.

Embrace the reflective energy of the Waning Gibbous in your gardening practices, and let its influence guide you in maintaining a healthy, well-organized garden. With thoughtful planning and attention to soil health and garden maintenance, you can create a garden that thrives through every phase of the lunar cycle, providing bountiful harvests and enduring beauty.

Chapter 32: Last Quarter: Release and Reduction

Introduction

The Last Quarter phase of the lunar cycle, occurring roughly three weeks after the New Moon, marks a period of release, reduction, and introspection. During this phase, the moon is half-illuminated, symbolizing a time for letting go and making necessary reductions in the garden. The Last Quarter is ideal for pruning, cutting back plants, and removing anything that is no longer serving the garden's health and productivity. Understanding the best practices for pruning and reducing during the Last Quarter can help gardeners maintain a balanced and thriving garden.

Understanding the Last Quarter's Influence on Gardening

The Last Quarter phase is characterized by a decrease in lunar energy, which signals a shift from growth and development to release and reflection. This phase encourages gardeners to focus on pruning, thinning, and reducing plant material to prepare the garden for the next lunar cycle. The Last Quarter is also an ideal time for removing weeds, managing pests, and addressing any garden issues that need resolution.

Key Benefits of Gardening During the Last Quarter:

- **Release and Reduction:** Encourages the removal of dead or unnecessary plant material to promote overall garden health.
- **Preparation for New Growth:** Helps prepare the garden for the next growth cycle by creating space and reducing competition.
- **Optimized Pruning:** Plants respond well to pruning during this phase, focusing on healing and redirecting energy.

Best Practices for Pruning and Reducing During the Last Quarter

To maximize the benefits of the Last Quarter phase, gardeners should engage in specific activities that align with this period of release and reduction.

Pruning and Cutting Back

Pruning and cutting back plants during the Last Quarter phase helps improve plant health, shape, and productivity. This phase is ideal for removing dead, damaged, or overgrown plant material.

1. **Pruning Techniques:**
   - **Deadheading:** Remove spent flowers and dead blooms to encourage further flowering and maintain plant aesthetics.
   - **Thinning:** Thin out crowded areas to improve air circulation and light penetration, reducing the risk of disease.
   - **Shaping:** Prune plants to maintain their desired shape and size, enhancing their appearance and health.
   - **Rejuvenation Pruning:** Cut back overgrown or leggy plants to rejuvenate them and encourage new growth.
2. **Tools and Equipment:**
   - **Pruning Shears:** Use clean, sharp pruning shears for precise cuts.
   - **Loppers:** Use loppers for thicker branches that require more force to cut.
   - **Pruning Saws:** Use pruning saws for large branches and woody stems.
3. **Pruning Guidelines:**
   - **Timing:** Prune during the early morning or late afternoon when temperatures are cooler and plants are less stressed.
   - **Technique:** Make clean, angled cuts just above a bud or node to promote healing and new growth.
   - **Disposal:** Remove and dispose of pruned material properly to prevent the spread of pests and diseases.

Reducing and Removing

Reducing and removing unnecessary plant material helps maintain garden health and prepares the space for future growth.

1. **Weed Removal:**
   - **Tasks:** Remove weeds and unwanted vegetation to reduce competition for nutrients and water.
   - **Benefits:** Helps maintain soil health and reduces the likelihood of weed problems in the next cycle.
2. **Removing Dead Plants:**
   - **Tasks:** Remove dead or dying plants, along with any remaining fruits or vegetables that are no longer viable.
   - **Benefits:** Prevents the spread of pests and diseases and frees up space for future planting.
3. **Clearing Debris:**
   - **Tasks:** Collect and dispose of garden debris, such as fallen leaves, twigs, and plant matter.
   - **Benefits:** Reduces the risk of pest infestations and creates a tidy, organized garden space.

Soil and Garden Maintenance

Maintaining the garden during the Last Quarter phase helps prepare the soil and garden infrastructure for the next planting cycle.

1. **Soil Preparation:**
   - **Tasks:** Incorporate compost, aged manure, and other organic matter into the soil to improve fertility and structure.
   - **Benefits:** Enhances soil health, promotes microbial activity, and improves water retention.
2. **Mulching:**
   - **Tasks:** Apply a layer of mulch to protect the soil, retain moisture, and suppress weeds.
   - **Benefits:** Helps maintain soil temperature, reduces erosion, and adds organic matter as it decomposes.

3. **Garden Infrastructure:**
    ◦ **Tasks:** Inspect and repair garden infrastructure, such as trellises, fences, and irrigation systems, to ensure they are ready for the next planting cycle.
    ◦ **Benefits:** Ensures a well-maintained garden environment, supporting healthy plant growth.

Practical Tips for Maximizing Last Quarter Gardening Success

To fully harness the benefits of the Last Quarter phase in gardening, consider the following practical tips:

Timing and Planning

1. **Lunar Calendar:** Use a lunar calendar to track the Last Quarter phase and plan your gardening activities accordingly. This phase typically lasts for about seven days, providing a window for optimal pruning and reducing.
2. **Weather Conditions:** Monitor weather forecasts and choose a day within the Last Quarter phase that offers favorable conditions for outdoor work.

Enhancing Soil Health

1. **Composting:** Start or maintain a compost pile to recycle garden waste and produce nutrient-rich compost for future use.
2. **Cover Crops:** Consider planting cover crops, such as clover or rye, to protect and enrich the soil during the off-season.

Garden Maintenance

1. **Tool Care:** Clean and sharpen gardening tools to ensure they are in good condition for future use.

2. **Pest and Disease Management:** Implement natural pest control methods and monitor plants for signs of disease to address issues promptly.

Examples of Successful Last Quarter Gardening

To illustrate the effectiveness of Last Quarter gardening, here are some examples of activities that thrive during this phase:

Pruning Shrubs and Trees

- **Benefits:** Pruning shrubs and trees during the Last Quarter phase helps maintain their shape, remove dead or diseased branches, and promote healthy growth. Plants respond well to pruning during this phase, focusing on healing and redirecting energy.

Weeding and Clearing Debris

- **Benefits:** Removing weeds and garden debris during the Last Quarter phase reduces competition for nutrients and water, improves soil health, and prevents pest infestations. A clean and tidy garden space is prepared for the next planting cycle.

Soil Amendment

- **Benefits:** Incorporating compost and organic matter into the soil during the Last Quarter phase improves soil structure, fertility, and water retention. This prepares the soil for the next planting cycle and promotes healthy plant growth.

Conclusion

The Last Quarter phase, with its focus on release and reduction, offers a unique opportunity for gardeners to maintain a balanced and thriving garden. By following best practices for pruning, reducing, soil enrichment, and garden maintenance, gardeners can ensure a smooth transition and prepare the garden for the next lunar cycle.

Embrace the reflective energy of the Last Quarter in your gardening practices, and let its influence guide you in maintaining a healthy, well-organized garden. With thoughtful planning and attention to soil health and garden maintenance, you can create a garden that thrives through every phase of the lunar cycle, providing bountiful harvests and enduring beauty.

Chapter 33: Waning Crescent: Rest and Renewal
Introduction

The Waning Crescent phase, the final stage of the lunar cycle, is characterized by a diminishing moon that is almost entirely in shadow. This phase represents a period of rest, renewal, and preparation for the new lunar cycle. For gardeners, the Waning Crescent is an ideal time for activities that focus on soil replenishment, garden maintenance, and restorative practices. Understanding the best practices for gardening during the Waning Crescent phase can help ensure a healthy, productive garden ready to embrace the next cycle of growth.

Understanding the Waning Crescent's Influence on Gardening

The Waning Crescent phase is characterized by a decrease in lunar energy, signaling a time for gardeners to rest, renew, and prepare the garden for future growth. This phase encourages activities that focus on soil health, garden cleanup, and planning for the upcoming planting cycle. The Waning Crescent is also a time for reflection and incorporating sustainable practices that promote long-term garden health.

Key Benefits of Gardening During the Waning Crescent:

- **Rest and Renewal:** Allows the garden to rest and regenerate, preparing for the new cycle.
- **Soil Replenishment:** Focuses on improving soil health and fertility.
- **Cleanup and Maintenance:** Emphasizes garden cleanup and maintenance to create a clean, organized space.
- **Planning and Reflection:** Provides an opportunity to reflect on past gardening practices and plan for future improvements.

Best Practices for Gardening During the Waning Crescent

To maximize the benefits of the Waning Crescent phase, gardeners should engage in specific activities that align with this period of rest and renewal.

Soil Replenishment and Health

Soil health is crucial for a productive garden. The Waning Crescent phase is ideal for activities that enhance soil fertility and structure.

1. **Adding Organic Matter:**
   - **Tasks:** Incorporate compost, aged manure, and other organic matter into the soil to improve fertility and structure.
   - **Benefits:** Enhances soil health, promotes microbial activity, and improves water retention.
2. **Cover Crops:**
   - **Tasks:** Plant cover crops such as clover, rye, or vetch to protect and enrich the soil during the off-season.
   - **Benefits:** Adds organic matter, prevents erosion, and improves soil structure.
3. **Soil Testing and Amendment:**
   - **Tasks:** Conduct soil tests to determine nutrient levels and pH balance. Add amendments as needed to correct deficiencies and create optimal growing conditions.
   - **Benefits:** Ensures that the soil is well-prepared for the next planting cycle and supports healthy plant growth.

Garden Cleanup and Maintenance

Cleaning up the garden during the Waning Crescent phase helps prepare the space for the next planting cycle and prevents the buildup of pests and diseases.

1. **Removing Spent Plants:**
   - **Tasks:** Remove dead or dying plants, along with any remaining fruits or vegetables that are no longer viable.
   - **Benefits:** Prevents the spread of pests and diseases and frees up space for future planting.
2. **Weeding:**
   - **Tasks:** Pull weeds and remove any unwanted vegetation to reduce competition for nutrients and water.
   - **Benefits:** Helps maintain soil health and reduces the likelihood of weed problems in the next cycle.
3. **Clearing Debris:**
   - **Tasks:** Collect and dispose of garden debris, such as fallen leaves, twigs, and plant matter.
   - **Benefits:** Reduces the risk of pest infestations and creates a tidy, organized garden space.

Restorative Practices

Engaging in restorative practices during the Waning Crescent phase helps rejuvenate the garden and prepare it for the next cycle.

1. **Composting:**
   - **Tasks:** Start or maintain a compost pile to recycle garden waste and produce nutrient-rich compost for future use.
   - **Benefits:** Enhances soil health, reduces waste, and provides a sustainable source of nutrients for the garden.
2. **Mulching:**
   - **Tasks:** Apply a layer of mulch to protect the soil, retain moisture, and suppress weeds.
   - **Benefits:** Helps maintain soil temperature, reduces erosion, and adds organic matter as it decomposes.
3. **Tool Maintenance:**
   - **Tasks:** Clean, sharpen, and repair gardening tools to ensure they are in good condition for future use.

- **Benefits:** Ensures tools are effective and ready for the next planting cycle, promoting efficient gardening practices.

Planning and Reflection

The Waning Crescent phase is an ideal time to reflect on past gardening practices, assess successes and challenges, and plan for future improvements.

1. **Garden Journal:**
   - **Tasks:** Record observations, successes, and challenges in a garden journal. Note the performance of different plants, weather conditions, and pest or disease issues.
   - **Benefits:** Provides valuable insights for future gardening practices and helps track progress over time.
2. **Planning Future Planting:**
   - **Tasks:** Plan the next planting cycle, considering crop rotation, companion planting, and garden layout. Select seeds and plants that align with your goals and growing conditions.
   - **Benefits:** Ensures a well-organized and efficient garden plan, maximizing space and resources.
3. **Reviewing and Learning:**
   - **Tasks:** Review gardening resources, such as books, articles, and online forums, to gather new ideas and techniques. Attend gardening workshops or join local gardening groups for additional insights.
   - **Benefits:** Enhances gardening knowledge and skills, leading to improved practices and better results.

Practical Tips for Maximizing Waning Crescent Gardening Success

To fully harness the benefits of the Waning Crescent phase in gardening, consider the following practical tips:

Timing and Planning

1. **Lunar Calendar:** Use a lunar calendar to track the Waning Crescent phase and plan your gardening activities accordingly. This phase typically lasts for about seven days, providing a window for optimal cleanup and preparation.
2. **Weather Conditions:** Monitor weather forecasts and choose a day within the Waning Crescent phase that offers favorable conditions for outdoor work.

Enhancing Soil Health

1. **Organic Amendments:** Incorporate organic amendments like compost, aged manure, and green manure crops to enrich the soil and promote healthy growth.
2. **Soil Testing:** Conduct soil tests to determine nutrient levels and pH balance. Adjust soil conditions as needed to provide an optimal growing environment for your plants.

Garden Maintenance

1. **Pest Control:** Implement natural pest control methods and monitor plants for signs of disease to address issues promptly.
2. **Tool Care:** Clean and sharpen gardening tools to ensure they are in good condition for future use.

Examples of Successful Waning Crescent Gardening

To illustrate the effectiveness of Waning Crescent gardening, here are some examples of activities that thrive during this phase:

Soil Amendment

- **Benefits:** Adding compost and organic matter to the soil during the Waning Crescent phase improves soil structure, fertility, and water retention. This prepares the soil for the next planting cycle and promotes healthy plant growth.

Composting

- **Benefits:** Starting or maintaining a compost pile during the Waning Crescent phase helps recycle garden waste and produce nutrient-rich compost for future use. The decomposing plant matter adds valuable organic matter to the soil.

Planning and Reflection

- **Benefits:** Reflecting on past gardening practices and planning for the future during the Waning Crescent phase helps ensure a well-organized and efficient garden layout. This maximizes space and resources and leads to improved gardening outcomes.

Conclusion

The Waning Crescent phase, with its focus on rest and renewal, offers a unique opportunity for gardeners to enhance soil health, maintain the garden, and prepare for the next cycle. By following best practices for soil replenishment, garden cleanup, restorative practices, and planning, gardeners can ensure a smooth transition and set the stage for continued success.

Embrace the reflective energy of the Waning Crescent in your gardening practices, and let its influence guide you in maintaining a healthy, well-organized garden. With thoughtful planning and attention to soil health and garden maintenance, you can create a garden that thrives through every phase of the lunar cycle, providing bountiful harvests and enduring beauty.

Part 5: Celestial Events and Gardening

Chapter 34: Solar Eclipses: Transformation and Change

Introduction

Solar eclipses, rare and powerful astronomical events, have long been associated with transformation and change. During a solar eclipse, the moon passes between the Earth and the sun, temporarily obscuring the sun's light. This phenomenon can have profound effects on both natural and human-made environments. For gardeners, solar eclipses represent a time of significant energy shifts, offering opportunities for transformation and renewal in the garden. Understanding how solar eclipses affect gardening and the best practices during these events can help gardeners harness this unique energy for positive change.

Understanding Solar Eclipses and Their Influence on Gardening

Solar eclipses occur when the moon aligns perfectly between the Earth and the sun, casting a shadow on the Earth and partially or completely blocking the sun's light. These events can be total, partial, or annular, depending on the alignment and distance of the moon. Solar eclipses bring about shifts in energy that can influence plant growth, soil health, and overall garden dynamics.

Key Effects of Solar Eclipses on Gardening:

- **Energy Shifts:** Solar eclipses create temporary disruptions in sunlight, impacting photosynthesis and plant energy cycles.
- **Soil and Water Dynamics:** The sudden change in light and temperature can affect soil moisture levels and water uptake in plants.

- **Symbolic Transformation:** Eclipses symbolize significant changes and transformations, encouraging gardeners to embrace renewal and adaptation.

Best Practices for Gardening During Solar Eclipses

To make the most of the transformative energy of solar eclipses, gardeners should engage in specific practices that align with the unique characteristics of these events.

Preparing for the Solar Eclipse

Proper preparation can help mitigate potential negative effects and enhance the positive impacts of a solar eclipse on the garden.

1. **Monitoring Eclipse Dates:**
   - **Tasks:** Keep track of upcoming solar eclipse dates using an astronomical calendar. Note the type (total, partial, annular) and duration of the eclipse.
   - **Benefits:** Being aware of eclipse dates allows for timely preparation and planning of gardening activities.
2. **Adjusting Watering Schedules:**
   - **Tasks:** Water plants thoroughly before the eclipse to ensure they are well-hydrated, as the temporary loss of sunlight can affect water uptake.
   - **Benefits:** Prevents stress on plants due to changes in light and temperature during the eclipse.

During the Solar Eclipse

During the eclipse, gardeners should focus on activities that support plant health and capitalize on the transformative energy of the event.

1. **Minimizing Stress on Plants:**
   - **Tasks:** Avoid major gardening activities such as pruning, transplanting, or fertilizing during the eclipse to reduce stress on plants.

- **Benefits:** Helps plants cope with the temporary disruption in sunlight and energy.

2. **Observing Plant Responses:**
   - **Tasks:** Observe how different plants respond to the eclipse. Note any changes in behavior, such as wilting, closing of flowers, or altered growth patterns.
   - **Benefits:** Provides valuable insights into plant resilience and adaptability, informing future gardening practices.
3. **Meditation and Reflection:**
   - **Tasks:** Use the eclipse as an opportunity for personal reflection and meditation in the garden. Focus on setting intentions for transformation and renewal.
   - **Benefits:** Enhances the gardener's connection with the garden and aligns personal energy with the transformative power of the eclipse.

Post-Eclipse Activities

After the eclipse, gardeners can engage in activities that promote renewal and capitalize on the new energy brought by the event.

1. **Assessing Plant Health:**
   - **Tasks:** Check plants for any signs of stress or damage caused by the eclipse. Address any issues promptly to promote recovery.
   - **Benefits:** Ensures that plants remain healthy and resilient after the eclipse.
2. **Pruning and Thinning:**
   - **Tasks:** Prune dead or damaged branches, thin out overcrowded areas, and remove any spent flowers or fruits.

- **Benefits:** Promotes healthy growth and allows plants to channel energy into new growth.

3. **Soil Replenishment:**
   - **Tasks:** Add compost, organic matter, and soil amendments to replenish nutrients and improve soil health.
   - **Benefits:** Enhances soil fertility and structure, supporting robust plant growth.

4. **Planting New Seeds:**
   - **Tasks:** Consider planting new seeds or transplanting seedlings shortly after the eclipse, using the symbolic energy of new beginnings and transformation.
   - **Benefits:** Capitalizes on the renewed energy to promote strong germination and growth.

Practical Tips for Maximizing Solar Eclipse Gardening Success

To fully harness the benefits of solar eclipses in gardening, consider the following practical tips:

Timing and Planning

1. **Astronomical Calendar:** Use an astronomical calendar to track upcoming solar eclipses and plan gardening activities accordingly.
2. **Weather Conditions:** Monitor weather forecasts and choose days around the eclipse that offer favorable conditions for gardening.

Enhancing Soil and Plant Health

1. **Organic Amendments:** Incorporate organic amendments like compost, aged manure, and green manure crops to enrich the soil and promote healthy growth.
2. **Soil Testing:** Conduct soil tests to determine nutrient levels and pH balance. Adjust soil conditions as needed to provide an optimal growing environment for your plants.

Garden Maintenance

1. **Tool Care:** Clean and sharpen gardening tools to ensure they are in good condition for post-eclipse activities.
2. **Pest Control:** Implement natural pest control methods and monitor plants for signs of disease to address issues promptly.

Examples of Successful Solar Eclipse Gardening

To illustrate the effectiveness of solar eclipse gardening, here are some examples of activities that thrive during this phase:

Soil Amendment

- **Benefits:** Adding compost and organic matter to the soil during the Waning Crescent phase improves soil structure, fertility, and water retention. This prepares the soil for the next planting cycle and promotes healthy plant growth.

Composting

- **Benefits:** Starting or maintaining a compost pile during the Waning Crescent phase helps recycle garden waste and produce nutrient-rich compost for future use. The decomposing plant matter adds valuable organic matter to the soil.

Planting New Seeds

- **Benefits:** Planting new seeds shortly after the eclipse capitalizes on the symbolic energy of new beginnings and transformation, promoting strong germination and growth.

Conclusion

Solar eclipses, with their focus on transformation and change, offer a unique opportunity for gardeners to enhance soil health, maintain the garden, and prepare for the next cycle. By following best practices for soil replenishment, garden cleanup, restorative practices, and planning, gardeners can ensure a smooth transition and set the stage for continued success.

Embrace the transformative energy of solar eclipses in your gardening practices, and let their influence guide you in maintaining a healthy, well-organized garden. With thoughtful planning and attention to soil health and garden maintenance, you can create a garden that thrives through every phase of the lunar cycle, providing bountiful harvests and enduring beauty.

Chapter 35: Lunar Eclipses: Reflection and Release
Introduction
Lunar eclipses, like their solar counterparts, are powerful astronomical events that have a significant impact on the natural world. During a lunar eclipse, the Earth comes between the sun and the moon, casting a shadow on the moon and often giving it a reddish hue. These events can be total, partial, or penumbral, each bringing unique effects. For gardeners, lunar eclipses represent a time for reflection, release, and renewal. Understanding how lunar eclipses affect gardening and the best practices during these periods can help harness their transformative energy to enhance garden health and productivity.

Understanding Lunar Eclipses and Their Influence on Gardening
Lunar eclipses occur when the Earth aligns directly between the sun and the moon, blocking sunlight from reaching the moon. This alignment results in the Earth's shadow falling on the moon, creating a temporary change in light and energy. Lunar eclipses symbolize a time of completion, introspection, and release, offering a unique opportunity for gardeners to let go of what no longer serves their garden and prepare for new growth.

Key Effects of Lunar Eclipses on Gardening:

- **Energy Shifts:** Lunar eclipses create temporary disruptions in light and energy, impacting plant cycles and growth.
- **Symbolic Release:** Eclipses symbolize letting go and making way for new beginnings, encouraging gardeners to remove old, diseased, or unproductive plant material.
- **Reflection and Introspection:** These events provide a time for gardeners to reflect on their practices, assess the garden's health, and plan for future improvements.

Best Practices for Gardening During Lunar Eclipses

To make the most of the reflective and releasing energy of lunar eclipses, gardeners should engage in specific practices that align with these periods.

Preparing for the Lunar Eclipse

Proper preparation can help mitigate potential negative effects and enhance the positive impacts of a lunar eclipse on the garden.

1. **Monitoring Eclipse Dates:**
   - **Tasks:** Keep track of upcoming lunar eclipse dates using an astronomical calendar. Note the type (total, partial, penumbral) and duration of the eclipse.
   - **Benefits:** Being aware of eclipse dates allows for timely preparation and planning of gardening activities.
2. **Adjusting Watering Schedules:**
   - **Tasks:** Water plants thoroughly before the eclipse to ensure they are well-hydrated, as the temporary change in light can affect water uptake.
   - **Benefits:** Prevents stress on plants due to changes in light and energy.

During the Lunar Eclipse

During the eclipse, gardeners should focus on activities that support plant health and capitalize on the reflective energy of the event.

1. **Minimizing Stress on Plants:**
   - **Tasks:** Avoid major gardening activities such as transplanting, fertilizing, or heavy pruning during the eclipse to reduce stress on plants.
   - **Benefits:** Helps plants cope with the temporary disruption in light and energy.

2. **Observing Plant Responses:**
   - **Tasks:** Observe how different plants respond to the eclipse. Note any changes in behavior, such as wilting, closing of flowers, or altered growth patterns.
   - **Benefits:** Provides valuable insights into plant resilience and adaptability, informing future gardening practices.
3. **Meditation and Reflection:**
   - **Tasks:** Use the eclipse as an opportunity for personal reflection and meditation in the garden. Focus on setting intentions for release and renewal.
   - **Benefits:** Enhances the gardener's connection with the garden and aligns personal energy with the transformative power of the eclipse.

Post-Eclipse Activities

After the eclipse, gardeners can engage in activities that promote release and capitalize on the new energy brought by the event.

1. **Pruning and Thinning:**
   - **Tasks:** Prune dead or damaged branches, thin out overcrowded areas, and remove any spent flowers or fruits.
   - **Benefits:** Promotes healthy growth and allows plants to channel energy into new growth.
2. **Removing Weeds and Debris:**
   - **Tasks:** Remove weeds, dead plants, and garden debris to create a clean, organized space.
   - **Benefits:** Reduces the risk of pests and diseases and prepares the garden for future planting.
3. **Soil Enrichment:**
   - **Tasks:** Add compost, organic matter, and soil amendments to replenish nutrients and improve soil health.
   - **Benefits:** Enhances soil fertility and structure, supporting robust plant growth.

4. **Planning and Reflection:**
    ◦ **Tasks:** Reflect on past gardening practices, assess successes and challenges, and plan for future improvements.
    ◦ **Benefits:** Provides valuable insights for future gardening practices and helps track progress over time.

Practical Tips for Maximizing Lunar Eclipse Gardening Success

To fully harness the benefits of lunar eclipses in gardening, consider the following practical tips:

Timing and Planning

1. **Astronomical Calendar:** Use an astronomical calendar to track upcoming lunar eclipses and plan gardening activities accordingly.
2. **Weather Conditions:** Monitor weather forecasts and choose days around the eclipse that offer favorable conditions for gardening.

Enhancing Soil and Plant Health

1. **Organic Amendments:** Incorporate organic amendments like compost, aged manure, and green manure crops to enrich the soil and promote healthy growth.
2. **Soil Testing:** Conduct soil tests to determine nutrient levels and pH balance. Adjust soil conditions as needed to provide an optimal growing environment for your plants.

Garden Maintenance

1. **Tool Care:** Clean and sharpen gardening tools to ensure they are in good condition for post-eclipse activities.

2. **Pest Control:** Implement natural pest control methods and monitor plants for signs of disease to address issues promptly.

Examples of Successful Lunar Eclipse Gardening

To illustrate the effectiveness of lunar eclipse gardening, here are some examples of activities that thrive during this phase:

Pruning Shrubs and Trees

- **Benefits:** Pruning shrubs and trees during the lunar eclipse phase helps maintain their shape, remove dead or diseased branches, and promote healthy growth. Plants respond well to pruning during this phase, focusing on healing and redirecting energy.

Removing Weeds and Debris

- **Benefits:** Removing weeds and garden debris during the lunar eclipse phase reduces competition for nutrients and water, improves soil health, and prevents pest infestations. A clean and tidy garden space is prepared for the next planting cycle.

Soil Amendment

- **Benefits:** Adding compost and organic matter to the soil during the lunar eclipse phase improves soil structure, fertility, and water retention. This prepares the soil for the next planting cycle and promotes healthy plant growth.

Conclusion

Lunar eclipses, with their focus on reflection and release, offer a unique opportunity for gardeners to enhance soil health, maintain the garden, and prepare for the next cycle. By following best practices for soil replenishment, garden cleanup, restorative practices, and planning, gardeners can ensure a smooth transition and set the stage for continued success.

Embrace the reflective energy of lunar eclipses in your gardening practices, and let their influence guide you in maintaining a healthy, well-organized garden. With thoughtful planning and attention to soil health and garden maintenance, you can create a garden that thrives through every phase of the lunar cycle, providing bountiful harvests and enduring beauty.

Chapter 36: Planetary Alignments: Harmony and Growth
Introduction
Planetary alignments, where multiple planets line up in the sky, have been historically regarded as events of significant astrological influence. These alignments, which occur when planets position themselves in a straight line relative to the Earth, can enhance or alter the energy dynamics in various aspects of life, including gardening. Understanding the influence of major planetary alignments on gardening and adopting optimal practices during these events can help gardeners harness this cosmic energy to promote harmony and growth in their gardens.

Understanding Planetary Alignments and Their Influence on Gardening

Planetary alignments occur when two or more planets appear close to each other in the sky from Earth's perspective. These events can amplify the energies of the involved planets, creating unique opportunities and challenges for gardening. The combined gravitational forces and energetic influences of these celestial bodies can impact plant growth, soil health, and overall garden dynamics.

Key Effects of Planetary Alignments on Gardening:

- **Enhanced Energies:** Planetary alignments can amplify the energies of the involved planets, promoting vigorous growth and harmonious development.
- **Gravitational Influence:** The combined gravitational pull of aligned planets can affect soil moisture and nutrient availability.
- **Symbolic Harmony:** Alignments symbolize balance and harmony, encouraging gardeners to focus on creating a balanced and cohesive garden environment.

Major Planetary Alignments and Their Gardening Influences
Different planetary alignments have unique influences based on the characteristics of the involved planets. Here are some examples of major alignments and their potential effects on gardening:

Jupiter and Saturn Conjunction (Great Conjunction)

- **Frequency:** Approximately every 20 years
- **Influence:** The conjunction of Jupiter and Saturn, known as the Great Conjunction, combines Jupiter's expansive and growth-promoting energy with Saturn's disciplined and structured influence.
- **Gardening Impact:** This alignment is ideal for long-term planning and the establishment of perennial gardens. It encourages gardeners to focus on sustainable practices and create well-structured, resilient garden spaces.

Mars and Venus Conjunction

- **Frequency:** Approximately every 2 years
- **Influence:** The conjunction of Mars and Venus blends Mars' energetic and action-oriented qualities with Venus' nurturing and beauty-enhancing attributes.
- **Gardening Impact:** This alignment is perfect for initiating new projects, planting flowering plants, and enhancing the aesthetic appeal of the garden. It promotes vigorous growth and vibrant blooms.

Mercury and Venus Conjunction

- **Frequency:** Several times a year
- **Influence:** The conjunction of Mercury and Venus combines Mercury's communication and adaptability with Venus' nurturing and harmonious energy.
- **Gardening Impact:** This alignment is ideal for improving plant communication through companion planting, enhancing soil health, and focusing on garden aesthetics. It encourages adaptability and flexibility in gardening practices.

Best Practices for Gardening During Planetary Alignments

To maximize the benefits of planetary alignments, gardeners should engage in specific practices that align with the unique characteristics of these events.

Preparing for Planetary Alignments

Proper preparation can help mitigate potential negative effects and enhance the positive impacts of planetary alignments on the garden.

1. **Monitoring Alignment Dates:**
   - **Tasks:** Keep track of upcoming planetary alignments using an astronomical calendar. Note the involved planets and the duration of the alignment.
   - **Benefits:** Being aware of alignment dates allows for timely preparation and planning of gardening activities.
2. **Adjusting Watering and Fertilizing Schedules:**
   - **Tasks:** Adjust watering and fertilizing schedules to ensure plants are well-hydrated and nourished before and during the alignment.

- **Benefits:** Prevents stress on plants due to changes in gravitational forces and energy dynamics.

During the Planetary Alignment

During the alignment, gardeners should focus on activities that support plant health and capitalize on the harmonious energy of the event.

1. **Planting and Transplanting:**
   - **Tasks:** Plant new seeds, transplant seedlings, and introduce new plants to the garden. Choose plants that align with the energies of the involved planets.
   - **Benefits:** Promotes strong germination, root development, and overall growth.
2. **Enhancing Soil Health:**
   - **Tasks:** Incorporate compost, organic matter, and soil amendments to enrich the soil and improve its structure.
   - **Benefits:** Enhances soil fertility, promotes microbial activity, and improves water retention.
3. **Pruning and Training:**
   - **Tasks:** Prune dead or damaged branches, thin out overcrowded areas, and train plants to grow in desired directions.
   - **Benefits:** Promotes healthy growth, improves air circulation, and enhances the garden's aesthetic appeal.

Post-Alignment Activities

After the alignment, gardeners can engage in activities that consolidate the gains made during the event and prepare for future growth.

1. **Assessing Plant Health:**
   - **Tasks:** Check plants for any signs of stress or damage caused by the alignment. Address any issues promptly to promote recovery.

- **Benefits:** Ensures that plants remain healthy and resilient after the alignment.

2. **Harvesting and Enjoying the Bounty:**
   - **Tasks:** Harvest mature crops and enjoy the fruits of your labor. Use this time to celebrate the garden's abundance and share it with others.
   - **Benefits:** Provides a sense of accomplishment and fulfillment, reinforcing the positive impact of the planetary alignment.

3. **Reflecting and Planning:**
   - **Tasks:** Reflect on the gardening activities conducted during the alignment, assess their outcomes, and plan for future improvements.
   - **Benefits:** Provides valuable insights for future gardening practices and helps track progress over time.

Practical Tips for Maximizing Planetary Alignment Gardening Success

To fully harness the benefits of planetary alignments in gardening, consider the following practical tips:

Timing and Planning

1. **Astronomical Calendar:** Use an astronomical calendar to track upcoming planetary alignments and plan gardening activities accordingly.
2. **Weather Conditions:** Monitor weather forecasts and choose days around the alignment that offer favorable conditions for gardening.

Enhancing Soil and Plant Health

1. **Organic Amendments:** Incorporate organic amendments like compost, aged manure, and green manure crops to enrich the soil and promote healthy growth.
2. **Soil Testing:** Conduct soil tests to determine nutrient levels and pH balance. Adjust soil conditions as needed to provide an optimal growing environment for your plants.

Garden Maintenance

1. **Tool Care:** Clean and sharpen gardening tools to ensure they are in good condition for post-alignment activities.
2. **Pest Control:** Implement natural pest control methods and monitor plants for signs of disease to address issues promptly.

Examples of Successful Planetary Alignment Gardening

To illustrate the effectiveness of planetary alignment gardening, here are some examples of activities that thrive during these events:

Planting Perennials During Jupiter and Saturn Conjunction

- **Benefits:** Planting perennials during the Jupiter and Saturn conjunction promotes long-term growth and resilience. The combined energies of expansion and structure support the establishment of a sustainable, well-organized garden.

Enhancing Garden Aesthetics During Mars and Venus Conjunction

- **Benefits:** Enhancing garden aesthetics during the Mars and Venus conjunction by planting flowering plants and adding decorative elements boosts the garden's visual appeal. The vibrant growth and blooms reflect the harmony and energy of the alignment.

Improving Soil Health During Mercury and Venus Conjunction

- **Benefits:** Improving soil health during the Mercury and Venus conjunction by adding compost and organic matter enhances soil fertility and structure. The combined energies of communication and nurturing promote a balanced, healthy garden environment.

Conclusion

Planetary alignments, with their focus on harmony and growth, offer unique opportunities for gardeners to enhance soil health, maintain the garden, and prepare for the next cycle. By following best practices for soil replenishment, garden cleanup, restorative practices, and planning, gardeners can ensure a smooth transition and set the stage for continued success.

Embrace the harmonious energy of planetary alignments in your gardening practices, and let their influence guide you in maintaining a healthy, well-organized garden. With thoughtful planning and attention to soil health and garden maintenance, you can create a garden that thrives through every phase of the lunar cycle, providing bountiful harvests and enduring beauty.

Chapter 37: Solar Flares: Energy and Disruption
Introduction

Solar flares, intense bursts of radiation from the sun, can have significant effects on Earth's atmosphere and electromagnetic fields. These powerful events, resulting from the release of magnetic energy stored in the sun's atmosphere, can disrupt communication systems, weather patterns, and even biological systems on Earth. For gardeners, solar flares represent both a source of energetic influence and potential disruption. Understanding how solar flares affect plant growth and soil health, along with adopting optimal practices during these events, can help mitigate their negative impacts and harness their energy for positive outcomes in the garden.

Understanding Solar Flares and Their Influence on Gardening

Solar flares occur when the sun's magnetic field lines suddenly reconfigure, releasing vast amounts of energy into space. This energy travels in the form of electromagnetic radiation, including X-rays and ultraviolet (UV) light. When these flares reach Earth, they can temporarily alter the planet's magnetic field and increase ionization in the atmosphere. The impact of solar flares on gardening primarily stems from their influence on atmospheric conditions, soil health, and plant physiological processes.

Key Effects of Solar Flares on Gardening:

- **Increased Radiation:** Solar flares increase the levels of UV and X-ray radiation reaching the Earth's surface, which can affect plant growth and soil microorganisms.

- **Electromagnetic Disruption:** Fluctuations in the Earth's magnetic field can influence plant navigation systems and stress responses.
- **Temperature Variations:** Solar flares can cause short-term changes in atmospheric temperature, impacting plant metabolism and soil moisture levels.

Impact of Solar Flares on Plant Growth

Solar flares can influence various aspects of plant growth, from photosynthesis to stress responses. Here are some of the primary ways in which solar flares affect plants:

Photosynthesis and UV Radiation

- **Enhanced UV Exposure:** Solar flares increase UV radiation levels, which can damage plant cells and hinder photosynthesis.
- **Stress Response:** Plants may activate stress responses, including the production of protective compounds like flavonoids and antioxidants, to mitigate UV damage.

Plant Navigation Systems

- **Magnetoreception:** Some plants use the Earth's magnetic field to orient their growth and development. Solar flares can disrupt these navigation systems, leading to altered growth patterns.

Temperature and Moisture Levels

- **Temperature Fluctuations:** Sudden changes in temperature caused by solar flares can impact plant metabolic processes, affecting growth rates and water uptake.
- **Soil Moisture:** Increased radiation and temperature variations can lead to changes in soil moisture levels, influencing plant hydration and nutrient absorption.

Impact of Solar Flares on Soil Health

Solar flares also affect soil health by influencing soil microorganisms and nutrient dynamics. Here are some key effects on soil:

Soil Microorganisms

- **Microbial Activity:** Increased UV radiation can reduce microbial activity in the soil, impacting nutrient cycling and soil fertility.
- **Microbial Diversity:** Changes in radiation levels can alter the composition of soil microbial communities, affecting plant-microbe interactions.

Nutrient Dynamics

- **Nutrient Availability:** Fluctuations in soil moisture and temperature can influence nutrient availability and uptake by plants.
- **Soil Structure:** Changes in soil temperature and moisture can impact soil structure, affecting root growth and water infiltration.

Best Practices for Gardening During Solar Flares

To mitigate the negative impacts of solar flares and harness their energy for positive outcomes, gardeners should adopt specific practices during these events.

Monitoring Solar Flare Activity

Proper monitoring and preparation can help mitigate potential negative effects and enhance the positive impacts of solar flares on the garden.

1. **Monitoring Solar Activity:**
    - **Tasks:** Keep track of solar flare activity using space weather forecasting tools and websites such as NASA's Space Weather Prediction Center.

- ◦ **Benefits:** Being aware of upcoming solar flares allows for timely preparation and planning of gardening activities.

2. **Adjusting Garden Practices:**
   - ◦ **Tasks:** Modify watering, shading, and fertilizing practices to protect plants from increased radiation and temperature fluctuations.
   - ◦ **Benefits:** Helps minimize stress on plants and soil during solar flare events.

Protecting Plants from UV Radiation

During periods of increased UV radiation caused by solar flares, gardeners can take steps to protect their plants and enhance their resilience.

1. **Using Shade Cloth:**
   - ◦ **Tasks:** Install shade cloth over vulnerable plants to reduce exposure to harmful UV rays.
   - ◦ **Benefits:** Provides protection from excessive radiation and helps maintain optimal growing conditions.

2. **Applying Organic Mulch:**
   - ◦ **Tasks:** Apply a layer of organic mulch around plants to regulate soil temperature, retain moisture, and protect soil microorganisms.
   - ◦ **Benefits:** Helps mitigate the impact of temperature fluctuations and radiation on soil health.

3. **Watering and Hydration:**
   - ◦ **Tasks:** Ensure consistent and adequate watering to help plants cope with increased radiation and temperature variations.
   - ◦ **Benefits:** Supports plant hydration and reduces stress during solar flare events.

Enhancing Soil Health and Resilience

Maintaining soil health during solar flare events is crucial for supporting plant growth and mitigating negative impacts.

1. **Adding Organic Matter:**
   - **Tasks:** Incorporate compost, aged manure, and other organic matter into the soil to improve fertility and structure.
   - **Benefits:** Enhances soil health, promotes microbial activity, and improves water retention.
2. **Monitoring Soil Moisture:**
   - **Tasks:** Regularly monitor soil moisture levels and adjust irrigation practices to maintain optimal hydration.
   - **Benefits:** Ensures that plants receive adequate water and supports soil health during periods of increased radiation.
3. **Using Soil Amendments:**
   - **Tasks:** Apply soil amendments such as biochar or vermicompost to enhance soil structure and nutrient availability.
   - **Benefits:** Improves soil resilience and supports healthy plant growth during and after solar flare events.

Observing and Reflecting

Taking time to observe plant and soil responses during solar flare events can provide valuable insights for future gardening practices.

1. **Recording Observations:**
   - **Tasks:** Keep a garden journal to record observations of plant behavior, soil conditions, and overall garden health during solar flare events.
   - **Benefits:** Provides valuable data for understanding the impact of solar flares and informing future gardening practices.

2. **Assessing Plant Health:**
    - **Tasks:** Assess plant health after solar flare events and address any issues promptly to promote recovery.
    - **Benefits:** Ensures that plants remain healthy and resilient, minimizing long-term impacts.

Practical Tips for Maximizing Solar Flare Gardening Success

To fully harness the benefits of solar flares in gardening, consider the following practical tips:

Timing and Planning

1. **Solar Forecasting:** Use space weather forecasting tools to track upcoming solar flares and plan gardening activities accordingly.
2. **Weather Conditions:** Monitor weather forecasts and choose days around the solar flare that offer favorable conditions for gardening.

Enhancing Soil and Plant Health

1. **Organic Amendments:** Incorporate organic amendments like compost, aged manure, and green manure crops to enrich the soil and promote healthy growth.
2. **Soil Testing:** Conduct soil tests to determine nutrient levels and pH balance. Adjust soil conditions as needed to provide an optimal growing environment for your plants.

Garden Maintenance

1. **Tool Care:** Clean and sharpen gardening tools to ensure they are in good condition for post-solar flare activities.
2. **Pest Control:** Implement natural pest control methods and monitor plants for signs of disease to address issues promptly.

Examples of Successful Solar Flare Gardening

To illustrate the effectiveness of solar flare gardening, here are some examples of activities that thrive during these events:

Using Shade Cloth to Protect Plants

- **Benefits:** Installing shade cloth over vulnerable plants during solar flare events reduces exposure to harmful UV rays, preventing damage and supporting healthy growth.

Enhancing Soil Health with Organic Mulch

- **Benefits:** Applying organic mulch around plants helps regulate soil temperature, retain moisture, and protect soil microorganisms, mitigating the impact of solar flares on soil health.

Recording Observations and Adjusting Practices

- **Benefits:** Keeping a garden journal to record observations during solar flare events provides valuable data for understanding their impact and informs future gardening practices.

Conclusion

Solar flares, with their focus on energy and disruption, offer unique opportunities and challenges for gardeners. By following best practices for soil replenishment, plant protection, garden maintenance, and planning, gardeners can mitigate the negative impacts of solar flares and harness their energy for positive outcomes.

Embrace the transformative energy of solar flares in your gardening practices, and let their influence guide you in maintaining a healthy, well-organized garden. With thoughtful planning and attention to soil health and plant resilience, you can create a garden that thrives through every phase of the lunar cycle, providing bountiful harvests and enduring beauty.

Chapter 38: Meteor Showers: Enrichment and Illumination

Introduction

Meteor showers, spectacular celestial events where numerous meteors streak across the night sky, have captivated humans for centuries. These showers occur when the Earth passes through the debris left by a comet or asteroid, resulting in a flurry of meteors. While meteor showers are primarily a visual spectacle, they also offer unique opportunities for gardeners to enhance soil enrichment and garden vitality. Understanding the impact of meteor showers on gardening and adopting optimal soil enrichment techniques during these periods can help harness the beneficial aspects of these cosmic events.

Understanding Meteor Showers and Their Influence on Gardening

Meteor showers occur when Earth's orbit intersects with the trail of debris left by a comet or asteroid. As these particles enter the Earth's atmosphere, they burn up, creating bright streaks of light. While the immediate impact of meteor showers on gardening is subtle, the long-term effects can be significant, particularly through the introduction of cosmic dust and minerals into the soil.

Key Effects of Meteor Showers on Gardening:

- **Soil Enrichment:** Meteor showers can introduce cosmic dust and minerals into the soil, enhancing its nutrient profile.
- **Atmospheric Changes:** The influx of particles can influence atmospheric conditions, potentially affecting weather patterns and plant growth.
- **Inspiration and Timing:** Meteor showers offer an opportune moment to engage in reflective gardening practices, aligning with cosmic rhythms.

Impact of Meteor Showers on Soil Enrichment

Meteor showers can subtly enhance soil enrichment by introducing trace minerals and elements from cosmic dust. These contributions, while minute, can have cumulative benefits for soil health and plant growth.

Introduction of Cosmic Dust and Minerals

- **Mineral Enrichment:** Cosmic dust from meteor showers can add trace minerals such as iron, magnesium, and calcium to the soil, which are essential for plant growth and development.
- **Soil Health:** The introduction of these minerals can improve soil fertility, structure, and microbial activity, promoting overall garden health.

Best Practices for Gardening During Meteor Showers

To maximize the benefits of meteor showers, gardeners should engage in specific practices that align with the unique characteristics of these events.

Preparing for Meteor Showers

Proper preparation can help maximize the positive impacts of meteor showers on the garden.

1. **Monitoring Meteor Shower Dates:**
   - **Tasks:** Keep track of upcoming meteor shower dates using an astronomical calendar. Note the peak times and duration of the shower.
   - **Benefits:** Being aware of meteor shower dates allows for timely preparation and planning of gardening activities.
2. **Adjusting Garden Practices:**
   - **Tasks:** Modify soil enrichment, watering, and planting schedules to align with the timing of meteor showers.
   - **Benefits:** Helps synchronize gardening practices with the influx of cosmic dust and minerals.

During the Meteor Shower

During the meteor shower, gardeners should focus on activities that support soil enrichment and capitalize on the cosmic energy of the event.

1. **Soil Enrichment Techniques:**
   - **Tasks:** Incorporate organic matter, compost, and mineral-rich amendments into the soil to enhance its nutrient profile.
   - **Benefits:** Improves soil fertility, structure, and microbial activity, promoting healthy plant growth.
2. **Watering and Moisture Management:**
   - **Tasks:** Ensure consistent and adequate watering to help integrate cosmic dust and minerals into the soil.
   - **Benefits:** Supports plant hydration and nutrient uptake during and after the meteor shower.
3. **Reflective Gardening Practices:**
   - **Tasks:** Use the time of the meteor shower for reflective gardening activities such as journaling, planning, and setting intentions for the garden.
   - **Benefits:** Enhances the gardener's connection with the garden and aligns personal energy with the cosmic event.

Post-Meteor Shower Activities

After the meteor shower, gardeners can engage in activities that consolidate the gains made during the event and prepare for future growth.

1. **Assessing Soil Health:**
   - **Tasks:** Check soil conditions and plant health to assess the impact of the meteor shower. Address any issues promptly to promote recovery.
   - **Benefits:** Ensures that plants remain healthy and resilient after the meteor shower.

2. **Enhancing Soil with Organic Matter:**
    ◦ **Tasks:** Continue to add compost, aged manure, and other organic matter to the soil to maintain and enhance its nutrient profile.
    ◦ **Benefits:** Supports long-term soil health and fertility.
3. **Planning Future Planting:**
    ◦ **Tasks:** Reflect on the gardening activities conducted during the meteor shower, assess their outcomes, and plan for future improvements.
    ◦ **Benefits:** Provides valuable insights for future gardening practices and helps track progress over time.

Practical Tips for Maximizing Meteor Shower Gardening Success

To fully harness the benefits of meteor showers in gardening, consider the following practical tips:

Timing and Planning

1. **Astronomical Calendar:** Use an astronomical calendar to track upcoming meteor showers and plan gardening activities accordingly.
2. **Weather Conditions:** Monitor weather forecasts and choose days around the meteor shower that offer favorable conditions for gardening.

Enhancing Soil Health

1. **Organic Amendments:** Incorporate organic amendments like compost, aged manure, and green manure crops to enrich the soil and promote healthy growth.
2. **Soil Testing:** Conduct soil tests to determine nutrient levels and pH balance. Adjust soil conditions as needed to provide an optimal growing environment for your plants.

Garden Maintenance

1. **Tool Care:** Clean and sharpen gardening tools to ensure they are in good condition for post-meteor shower activities.
2. **Pest Control:** Implement natural pest control methods and monitor plants for signs of disease to address issues promptly.

Examples of Successful Meteor Shower Gardening

To illustrate the effectiveness of meteor shower gardening, here are some examples of activities that thrive during these events:

Soil Enrichment with Organic Matter

- **Benefits:** Adding compost and organic matter to the soil during the meteor shower enhances soil fertility and structure, supporting healthy plant growth.

Reflective Gardening Practices

- **Benefits:** Using the time of the meteor shower for reflective gardening activities such as journaling and planning enhances the gardener's connection with the garden and aligns personal energy with the cosmic event.

Monitoring and Adjusting Soil Conditions

- **Benefits:** Regularly monitoring soil conditions and adjusting gardening practices based on observations helps ensure that plants receive optimal care and support during and after the meteor shower.

Conclusion

Meteor showers, with their focus on enrichment and illumination, offer unique opportunities for gardeners to enhance soil health, maintain the garden, and prepare for future growth. By following best practices for soil enrichment, reflective gardening, garden maintenance, and planning, gardeners can harness the beneficial aspects of these cosmic events for positive outcomes.

Embrace the enriching energy of meteor showers in your gardening practices, and let their influence guide you in maintaining a healthy, well-organized garden. With thoughtful planning and attention to soil health and plant resilience, you can create a garden that thrives through every phase of the lunar cycle, providing bountiful harvests and enduring beauty.

Chapter 39: Equinoxes: Balance and Renewal

Introduction

Equinoxes, occurring twice a year in spring and autumn, mark a period of balance and renewal. During the equinox, day and night are of equal length, symbolizing a harmonious equilibrium between light and darkness. For gardeners, the equinoxes represent a time of transition and opportunity, offering optimal conditions for various gardening activities. Understanding the best gardening practices during the Spring and Autumn Equinoxes can help gardeners harness this period of balance and renewal to enhance their garden's health and productivity.

Understanding Equinoxes and Their Influence on Gardening

The equinoxes occur when the sun is directly above the equator, resulting in nearly equal day and night lengths across the globe. These events signal the start of spring and autumn, bringing changes in temperature, light, and plant growth cycles. The Spring Equinox (around March 20-21) heralds the beginning of the growing season, while the Autumn Equinox (around September 22-23) signals the transition to harvest and preparation for winter.

Key Effects of Equinoxes on Gardening:

- **Balanced Light:** Equinoxes provide balanced light conditions, supporting both new growth and the winding down of the growing season.
- **Temperature Changes:** Spring and autumn equinoxes bring moderate temperatures, ideal for planting and harvesting.
- **Renewal and Transition:** These periods are perfect for starting new garden projects and preparing the garden for seasonal transitions.

Best Gardening Practices During the Spring Equinox

The Spring Equinox marks the beginning of the growing season, making it an ideal time for planting, soil preparation, and garden planning.

Planting and Transplanting

Spring Equinox is the perfect time to start new plants and transplant seedlings into the garden.

1. **Seed Starting:**
   - **Tasks:** Start seeds indoors for vegetables, herbs, and flowers. Use seed trays or pots with a high-quality seed starting mix.
   - **Benefits:** Provides a head start on the growing season, ensuring strong, healthy seedlings for transplanting.

2. **Transplanting Seedlings:**
   - **Tasks:** Transplant seedlings started indoors or purchased from nurseries into the garden. Ensure the soil is well-prepared and temperatures are consistently above freezing.
   - **Benefits:** Promotes vigorous growth and early establishment of plants in the garden.

3. **Direct Sowing:**
   - **Tasks:** Directly sow seeds of cold-tolerant crops such as peas, spinach, radishes, and lettuce into the garden.
   - **Benefits:** Takes advantage of the moderate temperatures and balanced light conditions for optimal germination and growth.

Soil Preparation and Enrichment

Spring is the time to prepare the soil for the upcoming growing season by enhancing its fertility and structure.

1. **Adding Compost and Organic Matter:**
   - **Tasks:** Incorporate compost, aged manure, and other organic matter into the soil to improve fertility and structure.
   - **Benefits:** Enhances soil health, promotes microbial activity, and improves water retention.
2. **Testing and Amending Soil:**
   - **Tasks:** Conduct soil tests to determine nutrient levels and pH balance. Add necessary amendments such as lime, sulfur, or specific fertilizers.
   - **Benefits:** Ensures optimal soil conditions for healthy plant growth.
3. **Mulching:**
   - **Tasks:** Apply a layer of mulch around newly planted seedlings to retain moisture, regulate soil temperature, and suppress weeds.
   - **Benefits:** Protects young plants and promotes a healthy growing environment.

Garden Planning and Design

Spring Equinox is an excellent time to plan and design the garden layout for the upcoming season.

1. **Garden Layout Planning:**
   - **Tasks:** Plan the garden layout, considering crop rotation, companion planting, and space requirements for different plants.

- **Benefits:** Maximizes space utilization, reduces pest and disease risks, and promotes healthy plant growth.

2. **Creating New Garden Beds:**
   - **Tasks:** Establish new garden beds or expand existing ones. Prepare the soil by tilling, adding compost, and defining bed boundaries.
   - **Benefits:** Increases growing space and provides opportunities for growing a wider variety of crops.

Best Gardening Practices During the Autumn Equinox

The Autumn Equinox marks the transition from the growing season to harvest and garden preparation for winter.

Harvesting and Preserving

Autumn Equinox is the time to harvest mature crops and preserve the garden's bounty.

1. **Harvesting Mature Crops:**
   - **Tasks:** Harvest vegetables, fruits, and herbs that have reached maturity. Focus on crops such as tomatoes, pumpkins, apples, and root vegetables.
   - **Benefits:** Ensures optimal flavor and nutrient content in harvested produce.

2. **Preserving the Harvest:**
   - **Tasks:** Preserve the garden's bounty through canning, drying, freezing, and fermenting. Store harvested produce in a cool, dark place.
   - **Benefits:** Extends the shelf life of produce and provides a supply of homegrown food throughout the winter.

Garden Cleanup and Maintenance

Autumn is the time to clean up the garden and prepare it for the winter months.

1. **Removing Spent Plants:**
   - **Tasks:** Remove dead or dying plants, along with any remaining fruits or vegetables that are no longer viable.
   - **Benefits:** Prevents the spread of pests and diseases and frees up space for cover crops or fall plantings.
2. **Weeding and Clearing Debris:**
   - **Tasks:** Pull weeds and remove garden debris such as fallen leaves, twigs, and plant matter.
   - **Benefits:** Reduces the risk of pest infestations and creates a tidy, organized garden space.
3. **Soil Care and Cover Crops:**
   - **Tasks:** Plant cover crops such as clover, rye, or vetch to protect and enrich the soil during the off-season.
   - **Benefits:** Adds organic matter, prevents erosion, and improves soil structure.

Preparing for Winter

The Autumn Equinox is the time to prepare the garden for the colder months ahead.

1. **Mulching and Protecting Plants:**
   - **Tasks:** Apply a thick layer of mulch around perennials, shrubs, and trees to insulate roots and protect against temperature fluctuations.
   - **Benefits:** Helps retain soil moisture, suppresses weeds, and protects plants from winter stress.

2. **Winterizing Garden Structures:**
     - **Tasks:** Inspect and repair garden structures such as fences, trellises, and raised beds. Clean and store tools and equipment.
     - **Benefits:** Ensures that garden infrastructure is in good condition for the next growing season.
3. **Planting Fall Crops:**
     - **Tasks:** Plant fall crops such as garlic, onions, and leafy greens that can withstand cooler temperatures.
     - **Benefits:** Extends the growing season and provides a harvest during the fall and winter months.

Practical Tips for Maximizing Equinox Gardening Success

To fully harness the benefits of the equinoxes in gardening, consider the following practical tips:

Timing and Planning

1. **Astronomical Calendar:** Use an astronomical calendar to track the Spring and Autumn Equinoxes and plan gardening activities accordingly.
2. **Weather Conditions:** Monitor weather forecasts and choose days around the equinox that offer favorable conditions for gardening.

Enhancing Soil and Plant Health

1. **Organic Amendments:** Incorporate organic amendments like compost, aged manure, and green manure crops to enrich the soil and promote healthy growth.
2. **Soil Testing:** Conduct soil tests to determine nutrient levels and pH balance. Adjust soil conditions as needed to provide an optimal growing environment for your plants.

Garden Maintenance

1. **Tool Care:** Clean and sharpen gardening tools to ensure they are in good condition for equinox activities.
2. **Pest Control:** Implement natural pest control methods and monitor plants for signs of disease to address issues promptly.

Examples of Successful Equinox Gardening

To illustrate the effectiveness of equinox gardening, here are some examples of activities that thrive during these periods:

Planting Spring Vegetables and Herbs

- **Benefits:** Planting vegetables and herbs during the Spring Equinox ensures strong, healthy seedlings and early establishment in the garden. The balanced light and moderate temperatures support optimal growth.

Harvesting and Preserving Fall Produce

- **Benefits:** Harvesting and preserving fall produce during the Autumn Equinox ensures that the garden's bounty is captured at its peak flavor and nutrient content. Preservation methods extend the shelf life of produce, providing a supply of homegrown food throughout the winter.

Enhancing Soil Health with Cover Crops

- **Benefits:** Planting cover crops during the Autumn Equinox protects and enriches the soil during the off-season. The added organic matter improves soil structure, fertility, and microbial activity.

Conclusion

The equinoxes, with their focus on balance and renewal, offer unique opportunities for gardeners to enhance soil health, maintain the garden, and prepare for seasonal transitions. By following best practices for soil enrichment, planting, harvesting, garden maintenance, and planning, gardeners can harness the beneficial aspects of these cosmic events for positive outcomes.

Embrace the balancing energy of the equinoxes in your gardening practices, and let their influence guide you in maintaining a healthy, well-organized garden. With thoughtful planning and attention to soil health and plant resilience, you can create a garden that thrives through every phase of the lunar cycle, providing bountiful harvests and enduring beauty.

Chapter 40: Solstices: Peak Energy and Transition

Introduction

Solstices, occurring twice a year in summer and winter, mark significant points in the Earth's orbit around the sun. The Summer Solstice, around June 21, is the longest day of the year, while the Winter Solstice, around December 21, is the shortest day of the year. These events symbolize peak energy and significant transitions in light and temperature. Understanding the unique influences of the Summer and Winter Solstices on gardening and adopting optimal practices during these periods can help gardeners make the most of these powerful seasonal shifts.

Understanding Solstices and Their Influence on Gardening

The solstices are characterized by extreme differences in day length and solar energy. The Summer Solstice brings the most daylight and the highest solar energy, promoting vigorous plant growth. In contrast, the Winter Solstice has the least daylight, signaling a period of dormancy and preparation for renewal. Both solstices offer unique opportunities for specific gardening activities.

Key Effects of Solstices on Gardening:

- **Summer Solstice:** Peak solar energy and long daylight hours support robust plant growth, flowering, and fruiting.
- **Winter Solstice:** Minimal daylight and lower temperatures mark a time for rest, reflection, and preparation for the growing season.

Best Gardening Practices During the Summer Solstice

The Summer Solstice, with its peak energy and extended daylight, is ideal for activities that enhance growth, manage plant health, and prepare for the harvest.

Enhancing Plant Growth and Health

1. **Intensive Plant Care:**
   - **Tasks:** Regularly water and fertilize plants to support their vigorous growth during peak energy. Monitor for signs of nutrient deficiencies and pests.
   - **Benefits:** Ensures plants receive the nutrients and hydration they need to thrive during the period of maximum growth.
2. **Pruning and Training:**
   - **Tasks:** Prune plants to remove dead or diseased branches, shape growth, and improve air circulation. Train climbing plants on trellises or supports.
   - **Benefits:** Promotes healthy growth, prevents disease, and maximizes space utilization.
3. **Mulching:**
   - **Tasks:** Apply a thick layer of mulch around plants to retain moisture, regulate soil temperature, and suppress weeds.
   - **Benefits:** Protects soil moisture levels and reduces competition from weeds.

Managing Heat and Sunlight

1. **Shade Management:**
   - **Tasks:** Use shade cloth or plant taller crops to provide shade for sensitive plants during the hottest part of the day.
   - **Benefits:** Prevents heat stress and sunburn on delicate plants.
2. **Efficient Watering:**
   - **Tasks:** Implement drip irrigation or soaker hoses to deliver water directly to plant roots. Water early in the morning or late in the evening to minimize evaporation.

- **Benefits:** Ensures efficient water use and reduces water stress on plants.
3. **Planting Heat-Tolerant Crops:**
    - **Tasks:** Plant crops that thrive in high temperatures, such as tomatoes, peppers, eggplants, and squash.
    - **Benefits:** Takes advantage of peak summer conditions for optimal growth and yield.

Preparing for the Harvest

1. **Monitoring Crop Maturity:**
    - **Tasks:** Regularly check crops for signs of maturity and readiness for harvest. Harvest fruits and vegetables at their peak ripeness for best flavor and nutrition.
    - **Benefits:** Ensures optimal quality and maximizes yield.
2. **Preserving Produce:**
    - **Tasks:** Begin preserving excess produce through canning, drying, or freezing. Store harvested crops in a cool, dry place.
    - **Benefits:** Extends the shelf life of produce and reduces waste.

Best Gardening Practices During the Winter Solstice

The Winter Solstice, with its minimal daylight and lower temperatures, is ideal for activities that focus on rest, reflection, and preparation for the next growing season.

Garden Cleanup and Maintenance

1. **Removing Dead Plants:**
    - **Tasks:** Remove any remaining dead or diseased plants from the garden. Clear fallen leaves and debris.
    - **Benefits:** Reduces the risk of pests and diseases overwintering in the garden.

2. **Weeding and Soil Care:**
   - ◦ **Tasks:** Weed the garden to reduce competition for nutrients and water. Add compost and organic matter to enrich the soil.
   - ◦ **Benefits:** Improves soil fertility and prepares the garden for spring planting.
3. **Tool Maintenance:**
   - ◦ **Tasks:** Clean, sharpen, and repair gardening tools. Store them properly to prevent rust and damage.
   - ◦ **Benefits:** Ensures tools are ready for use in the next growing season.

Planning and Reflection

1. **Garden Journal:**
   - ◦ **Tasks:** Reflect on the past gardening season by reviewing notes and observations in a garden journal. Document successes, challenges, and lessons learned.
   - ◦ **Benefits:** Provides valuable insights for planning future gardening activities.
2. **Planning the Next Season:**
   - ◦ **Tasks:** Plan the layout and crops for the next growing season. Order seeds and supplies early to ensure availability.
   - ◦ **Benefits:** Helps create a well-organized and efficient garden plan.
3. **Designing New Garden Projects:**
   - ◦ **Tasks:** Design new garden beds, structures, or features. Consider implementing new gardening techniques or practices.
   - ◦ **Benefits:** Enhances the garden's aesthetics and functionality.

Protecting Plants and Soil

1. **Mulching and Covering:**
   - ◦ **Tasks:** Apply mulch around perennials and other overwintering plants to insulate roots and retain soil moisture. Use row covers or cold frames to protect sensitive plants.
   - ◦ **Benefits:** Protects plants from temperature fluctuations and harsh weather conditions.
2. **Planting Cover Crops:**
   - ◦ **Tasks:** Plant cover crops such as clover, rye, or vetch to protect and enrich the soil during the winter months.
   - ◦ **Benefits:** Prevents erosion, adds organic matter, and improves soil structure.
3. **Winter Sowing:**
   - ◦ **Tasks:** Use the winter sowing method to start hardy seeds outdoors in containers. This method takes advantage of natural temperature fluctuations to simulate natural germination cycles.
   - ◦ **Benefits:** Provides an early start for spring crops and requires minimal indoor space.

Practical Tips for Maximizing Solstice Gardening Success

To fully harness the benefits of the solstices in gardening, consider the following practical tips:

Timing and Planning

1. **Astronomical Calendar:** Use an astronomical calendar to track the Summer and Winter Solstices and plan gardening activities accordingly.

2. **Weather Conditions:** Monitor weather forecasts and choose days around the solstice that offer favorable conditions for gardening.

Enhancing Soil and Plant Health

1. **Organic Amendments:** Incorporate organic amendments like compost, aged manure, and green manure crops to enrich the soil and promote healthy growth.
2. **Soil Testing:** Conduct soil tests to determine nutrient levels and pH balance. Adjust soil conditions as needed to provide an optimal growing environment for your plants.

Garden Maintenance

1. **Tool Care:** Clean and sharpen gardening tools to ensure they are in good condition for solstice activities.
2. **Pest Control:** Implement natural pest control methods and monitor plants for signs of disease to address issues promptly.

Examples of Successful Solstice Gardening

To illustrate the effectiveness of solstice gardening, here are some examples of activities that thrive during these periods:

Intensive Summer Care for Heat-Loving Plants

- **Benefits:** Providing intensive care for heat-loving plants during the Summer Solstice ensures they receive the nutrients and hydration needed to thrive during peak growth conditions.

Winter Garden Planning and Soil Enrichment

- **Benefits:** Using the Winter Solstice for garden planning and soil enrichment activities prepares the garden for the next growing season and improves soil health.

Planting Cover Crops During the Winter Solstice

- **Benefits:** Planting cover crops during the Winter Solstice protects and enriches the soil, preventing erosion and adding organic matter for the next growing season.

Conclusion

The solstices, with their focus on peak energy and transition, offer unique opportunities for gardeners to enhance soil health, maintain the garden, and prepare for seasonal shifts. By following best practices for intensive care, planting, harvesting, garden maintenance, and planning, gardeners can harness the beneficial aspects of these cosmic events for positive outcomes.

Embrace the dynamic energy of the solstices in your gardening practices, and let their influence guide you in maintaining a healthy, well-organized garden. With thoughtful planning and attention to soil health and plant resilience, you can create a garden that thrives through every phase of the lunar cycle, providing bountiful harvests and enduring beauty.

Conclusion

Chapter 41: Integrating Astrology into Your Gardening Routine

Introduction

Integrating astrology into your gardening routine offers a holistic approach to cultivating a thriving garden. By aligning gardening practices with celestial cycles and astrological principles, you can enhance plant health, improve soil fertility, and create a harmonious garden environment. This chapter summarizes the key concepts and practical steps for incorporating astrological knowledge into your gardening activities, helping you harness the power of the stars for optimal garden success.

Understanding Astrological Principles and Gardening

Astrology provides a framework for understanding the influence of celestial bodies on earthly activities. In gardening, astrological principles can guide planting, harvesting, and maintenance practices to align with cosmic rhythms. Key astrological elements relevant to gardening include:

Lunar Phases

- **New Moon:** Ideal for planting seeds, starting new projects, and initiating growth.
- **Waxing Crescent:** Focus on growth and expansion, transplanting seedlings, and nurturing young plants.
- **First Quarter:** Strengthen plant growth, prune, and train plants for optimal development.
- **Waxing Gibbous:** Prepare for flowering and fruiting, enhance soil health, and ensure plant vitality.
- **Full Moon:** Harvest crops at peak potency, engage in significant garden projects, and celebrate abundance.
- **Waning Gibbous:** Reflect, complete harvesting, and clean up the garden.

- **Last Quarter:** Prune, reduce, and remove dead plant material to prepare for new growth.
- **Waning Crescent:** Rest, renew, and replenish soil for the next cycle.

Zodiac Signs

Each zodiac sign is associated with specific elemental qualities (fire, earth, air, water) and influences different aspects of plant growth and gardening activities.

- **Fire Signs (Aries, Leo, Sagittarius):** Promote vigorous growth, flowering, and fruiting.
- **Earth Signs (Taurus, Virgo, Capricorn):** Support root development, stability, and nourishment.
- **Air Signs (Gemini, Libra, Aquarius):** Enhance communication, balance, and aerial growth.
- **Water Signs (Cancer, Scorpio, Pisces):** Promote moisture retention, intuition, and sensitivity.

Practical Steps for Integrating Astrology into Gardening

To integrate astrological knowledge into your gardening routine, follow these practical steps:

1. Planning and Timing

Use an astrological calendar to plan your gardening activities according to lunar phases, zodiac signs, and celestial events.

- **Lunar Calendar:** Track lunar phases to schedule planting, watering, fertilizing, and harvesting activities.
- **Zodiac Calendar:** Align specific gardening tasks with the astrological influences of the zodiac signs.

2. Planting and Transplanting

Schedule planting and transplanting activities according to lunar phases and zodiac influences.

- **New Moon:** Plant seeds and start new projects.
- **Waxing Crescent:** Transplant seedlings and nurture young plants.
- **Full Moon:** Plant flowering and fruiting plants for optimal growth.

3. Soil Health and Enrichment

Enhance soil fertility and structure by aligning soil enrichment activities with lunar phases and zodiac signs.

- **Earth Signs:** Incorporate compost, organic matter, and soil amendments during earth sign phases for optimal root development and soil health.
- **Waxing Gibbous:** Add compost and organic fertilizers to support plant vitality.

4. Pruning and Training

Prune and train plants according to lunar phases to promote healthy growth and structure.

- **First Quarter:** Prune and train plants for strength and stability.
- **Last Quarter:** Prune dead or diseased branches to prepare for new growth.

5. Harvesting and Preserving

Harvest crops at their peak potency by aligning harvesting activities with lunar phases.

- **Full Moon:** Harvest crops for optimal flavor, nutrition, and potency.
- **Waning Gibbous:** Complete harvesting and begin preserving produce.

6. Reflective and Restorative Practices

Use the reflective energy of certain lunar phases to engage in garden maintenance, planning, and rest.

- **Waning Crescent:** Reflect, plan, and prepare the garden for the next cycle.
- **Winter Solstice:** Plan for the next growing season, enrich soil, and protect plants.

Examples of Integrated Astrological Gardening Practices

To illustrate the integration of astrological principles into gardening, here are some examples of practical applications:

Example 1: Planting Tomatoes

- **Timing:** Plant tomato seeds during the New Moon in a water sign for moisture retention and growth.
- **Transplanting:** Transplant seedlings during the Waxing Crescent in a fire sign for vigorous growth.
- **Fertilizing:** Apply organic fertilizers during the First Quarter in an earth sign for strong root development.

Example 2: Harvesting Herbs

- **Timing:** Harvest herbs during the Full Moon for peak potency and flavor.
- **Preserving:** Begin drying and preserving herbs during the Waning Gibbous to extend their shelf life.

Example 3: Pruning and Training Roses

- **Timing:** Prune roses during the First Quarter in an air sign for balanced growth and structure.
- **Training:** Train climbing roses on trellises during the Waxing Crescent in a fire sign for vigorous vertical growth.

Enhancing Garden Health with Celestial Events

In addition to lunar phases and zodiac signs, other celestial events such as solar and lunar eclipses, planetary alignments, and meteor showers offer unique opportunities for garden enrichment.

Solar Eclipses

- **Activities:** Use solar eclipses for transformation and change. Reflect on garden practices, plan new projects, and prepare for renewal.

Lunar Eclipses

- **Activities:** Focus on reflection and release. Prune, remove dead material, and prepare for new growth.

Planetary Alignments

- **Activities:** Use planetary alignments for harmony and growth. Enhance soil health, plant new crops, and promote balanced garden development.

Meteor Showers

- **Activities:** Enrich soil with organic matter during meteor showers to harness cosmic dust and minerals. Engage in reflective gardening practices.

Conclusion

Integrating astrology into your gardening routine offers a holistic approach that aligns your practices with cosmic rhythms and celestial cycles. By understanding and applying astrological principles, you can enhance plant health, improve soil fertility, and create a harmonious garden environment.

Embrace the power of the stars in your gardening practices, and let their influence guide you in maintaining a healthy, well-organized garden. With thoughtful planning, attention to soil health, and alignment with celestial events, you can create a garden that thrives through every phase of the lunar cycle, providing bountiful harvests and enduring beauty.

Chapter 42: Advanced Techniques and Future Trends

Introduction

Astrological gardening is an evolving field that combines traditional horticultural practices with astrological knowledge to create a holistic approach to gardening. As more gardeners discover the benefits of integrating celestial cycles into their gardening routines, advanced techniques and future trends continue to emerge. This chapter explores these advanced techniques and predicts future trends in astrological gardening, providing insights into how this practice will develop and how gardeners can stay ahead of the curve.

Advanced Techniques in Astrological Gardening

Integrating advanced astrological techniques into gardening can enhance productivity, plant health, and garden harmony. These methods build on basic astrological principles and incorporate innovative practices and technologies.

1. Biodynamic Gardening

Biodynamic gardening is an advanced approach that incorporates astrological principles, organic farming, and holistic practices to create self-sustaining ecosystems.

- **Planting by Lunar Phases:** Follow a biodynamic calendar to plant, transplant, and harvest crops according to lunar phases.
- **Biodynamic Preparations:** Use specially prepared herbal and mineral composts to enhance soil fertility and plant health.
- **Ecosystem Integration:** Integrate livestock, beneficial insects, and companion planting to create a balanced and self-sustaining garden ecosystem.

2. Astrological Pest Management

Advanced pest management techniques align with astrological cycles to minimize pest problems and enhance plant resilience.

- **Moon Phases and Pest Control:** Apply natural pest control methods during specific lunar phases for maximum effectiveness. For example, treat pests during the Full Moon when plant sap is high and pests are most active.
- **Zodiac Signs and Pest Activity:** Monitor pest activity according to zodiac signs. Earth signs can indicate increased soil-dwelling pests, while air signs may signal a rise in flying insects.

3. Precision Astrological Scheduling

Utilize advanced scheduling techniques to align gardening tasks with precise astrological timings for optimal results.

- **Ephemeris Use:** Employ an ephemeris, a table listing the positions of celestial bodies, to plan gardening activities with greater accuracy.
- **Planetary Hours:** Incorporate planetary hours into your gardening routine. Each hour of the day is ruled by a different planet, influencing specific gardening tasks. For example, water plants during a Moon hour for better hydration.

4. Astrological Soil Amendments

Enhance soil health by incorporating astrological principles into soil amendment practices.

- **Cosmic Dust Enrichment:** Use cosmic dust collected during meteor showers as a soil amendment to introduce trace minerals and enhance soil fertility.

- **Lunar Charged Water:** Water plants with lunar-charged water, which has been exposed to moonlight during specific lunar phases, to improve plant vitality and growth.

Future Trends in Astrological Gardening

The future of astrological gardening will likely see increased integration with technology, greater community engagement, and the development of new methods and practices.

1. Technological Integration

Technology will play a significant role in advancing astrological gardening practices, making it easier for gardeners to align their activities with celestial cycles.

- **Astrological Gardening Apps:** Development of mobile apps that provide real-time astrological data, personalized gardening calendars, and reminders for specific gardening tasks based on lunar phases and zodiac signs.
- **Smart Garden Systems:** Integration of astrological data into smart garden systems, which use sensors and automation to optimize watering, fertilizing, and pest control based on celestial influences.

2. Community Engagement and Education

Increased awareness and interest in astrological gardening will foster greater community engagement and educational opportunities.

- **Workshops and Courses:** More workshops, online courses, and seminars will be available to teach gardeners about astrological gardening principles and practices.
- **Community Gardens:** Establishment of community gardens that incorporate astrological gardening techniques, allowing gardeners to share knowledge and collaborate on astrological gardening projects.

3. Research and Development

Ongoing research and development will continue to refine and expand astrological gardening practices.

- **Scientific Studies:** Increased scientific studies on the effects of lunar phases, zodiac signs, and celestial events on plant growth and soil health will provide empirical support for astrological gardening practices.
- **New Techniques:** Development of new techniques and methods that integrate astrological principles with sustainable gardening practices, such as permaculture and regenerative agriculture.

4. Global Adaptation

As interest in astrological gardening grows, practices will be adapted to different climates, cultures, and agricultural systems worldwide.

- **Cultural Integration:** Integration of local astrological and agricultural traditions with modern astrological gardening practices, creating unique and region-specific approaches.
- **Climate-Specific Practices:** Adaptation of astrological gardening techniques to various climate conditions, ensuring their effectiveness in diverse environments.

Case Study: Astrological Gardening in Urban Environments
Background

An urban community garden in New York City decided to integrate advanced astrological gardening techniques to enhance productivity and engage the local community.

Implementation

The community garden team implemented several advanced techniques, including biodynamic practices, precision scheduling, and technological integration.

- **Biodynamic Practices:** The team followed a biodynamic calendar, used herbal and mineral composts, and integrated livestock and beneficial insects.
- **Precision Scheduling:** They employed an ephemeris and incorporated planetary hours into their gardening routine.
- **Technological Integration:** The garden used a mobile app to track lunar phases and zodiac signs, providing real-time data and personalized reminders.

Results

The community garden experienced significant improvements in productivity, plant health, and community engagement.

- **Increased Yield:** The garden saw a 50% increase in crop yields, with healthier and more resilient plants.
- **Enhanced Soil Health:** Biodynamic practices and astrological soil amendments improved soil fertility and structure.
- **Community Involvement:** Workshops and events attracted more participants, fostering a strong sense of community and shared knowledge.

Conclusion

Advanced techniques and future trends in astrological gardening offer exciting opportunities for gardeners to enhance their practices and achieve greater success. By integrating biodynamic principles, precision scheduling, technological advancements, and community engagement, gardeners can create thriving, harmonious gardens that align with celestial cycles.

Embrace these advanced techniques and stay informed about emerging trends to remain at the forefront of astrological gardening. With thoughtful planning, continuous learning, and a holistic approach, you can harness the power of the stars to create a garden that flourishes through every phase of the lunar cycle, providing abundant harvests and enduring beauty.

Chapter 43: Conclusion and Final Thoughts

Introduction

As we conclude our exploration of astrological gardening, it's essential to reflect on the synergy between astrology and gardening, the profound benefits it brings, and the potential it holds for future gardening practices. This final chapter provides an overview of the key concepts discussed, the holistic nature of integrating astrology into gardening, and encouragement for readers to experiment with these practices and share their experiences.

The Synergy Between Astrology and Gardening

Astrology and gardening, two ancient practices, are harmoniously intertwined when combined thoughtfully. This synergy offers a unique approach to understanding and enhancing the natural rhythms of the garden.

Understanding Natural Rhythms

Astrology provides a framework for understanding the natural rhythms and cycles that influence plant growth, soil health, and garden vitality. By aligning gardening practices with celestial cycles, gardeners can:

- **Optimize Planting and Harvesting:** Aligning planting and harvesting activities with lunar phases and zodiac signs can enhance growth, yield, and potency of crops.
- **Enhance Soil Health:** Utilizing celestial events and astrological principles to time soil enrichment and maintenance activities improves soil fertility and structure.
- **Promote Garden Harmony:** Integrating astrology into garden planning and maintenance fosters a balanced and harmonious environment, supporting overall garden health.

Holistic Approach to Gardening

Astrological gardening promotes a holistic approach that considers not just the physical aspects of gardening but also the energetic and spiritual dimensions.

- **Connection to Nature:** Astrological gardening deepens the gardener's connection to the natural world, fostering a sense of harmony and balance with the earth and celestial bodies.
- **Intuitive Practices:** Encourages gardeners to develop and trust their intuition, aligning their actions with the natural rhythms and energies present in their garden.
- **Sustainable Gardening:** Emphasizes sustainable and regenerative practices that work in harmony with natural cycles, promoting long-term garden health and productivity.

Key Concepts and Practices

Throughout this book, we have explored various aspects of astrological gardening, providing practical guidance and detailed explanations of how to integrate astrological principles into your gardening routine.

Lunar Phases

- **New Moon:** Ideal for planting seeds and initiating new projects.
- **Waxing Crescent:** Focus on growth and expansion, transplanting seedlings, and nurturing young plants.
- **First Quarter:** Strengthen plant growth, prune, and train plants for optimal development.
- **Waxing Gibbous:** Prepare for flowering and fruiting, enhance soil health, and ensure plant vitality.
- **Full Moon:** Harvest crops at peak potency, engage in significant garden projects, and celebrate abundance.
- **Waning Gibbous:** Reflect, complete harvesting, and clean up the garden.

- **Last Quarter:** Prune, reduce, and remove dead plant material to prepare for new growth.
- **Waning Crescent:** Rest, renew, and replenish soil for the next cycle.

Zodiac Signs

Each zodiac sign influences specific aspects of plant growth and gardening activities.

- **Fire Signs (Aries, Leo, Sagittarius):** Promote vigorous growth, flowering, and fruiting.
- **Earth Signs (Taurus, Virgo, Capricorn):** Support root development, stability, and nourishment.
- **Air Signs (Gemini, Libra, Aquarius):** Enhance communication, balance, and aerial growth.
- **Water Signs (Cancer, Scorpio, Pisces):** Promote moisture retention, intuition, and sensitivity.

Celestial Events

Leveraging celestial events such as solar and lunar eclipses, planetary alignments, and meteor showers can further enhance garden productivity and health.

- **Solar Eclipses:** Use for transformation and change, reflecting on garden practices and planning new projects.
- **Lunar Eclipses:** Focus on reflection and release, pruning, and preparing for new growth.
- **Planetary Alignments:** Enhance soil health, plant new crops, and promote balanced garden development.
- **Meteor Showers:** Enrich soil with cosmic dust and minerals, engage in reflective gardening practices.

Encouragement to Experiment and Share

Astrological gardening is a dynamic and evolving practice that benefits from experimentation and shared experiences. As you embark on your journey of integrating astrology into your gardening routine, consider the following:

Experiment and Observe

- **Personalize Your Practice:** Tailor astrological gardening practices to suit your specific garden conditions, climate, and plant preferences.
- **Keep a Garden Journal:** Document your gardening activities, observations, and results. Note how different lunar phases, zodiac signs, and celestial events impact your garden.
- **Be Open to Change:** Gardening is an iterative process. Be willing to adapt and modify your practices based on your observations and experiences.

Share Your Experiences

- **Join Gardening Communities:** Participate in local or online gardening communities to share your experiences and learn from others.
- **Teach and Inspire:** Share your knowledge and experiences with friends, family, and fellow gardeners. Consider hosting workshops or writing articles to inspire others to explore astrological gardening.
- **Celebrate Successes:** Celebrate your gardening successes, both big and small. Share your achievements with your community to foster a sense of connection and shared purpose.

Final Thoughts

Astrological gardening offers a profound and enriching approach to cultivating a thriving garden. By aligning your gardening practices with celestial cycles, you can enhance plant health, improve soil fertility, and create a harmonious garden environment. The journey of integrating astrology into gardening is one of continuous learning, experimentation, and reflection.

Embrace the synergy between astrology and gardening, and let the wisdom of the stars guide you in creating a garden that flourishes through every phase of the lunar cycle. As you experiment and share your experiences, you contribute to the growing body of knowledge and inspire others to explore this holistic and harmonious approach to gardening.

With thoughtful planning, attention to detail, and a deep connection to the natural world, you can create a garden that provides bountiful harvests, enduring beauty, and a profound sense of fulfillment. May your gardening journey be guided by the stars and enriched by the rhythms of the cosmos.

Appendices

Appendix A: Glossary

This glossary provides definitions of key terms used throughout the book, covering both gardening and astrological concepts. Understanding these terms will help you better integrate astrological principles into your gardening practices.

Gardening Terms

Annuals: Plants that complete their life cycle, from germination to seed production, within one growing season.

Biennials: Plants that require two growing seasons to complete their life cycle, typically growing vegetative structures in the first year and flowering in the second.

Biodynamic Gardening: An advanced form of organic gardening that incorporates astrological principles, herbal and mineral composts, and holistic practices to create a self-sustaining ecosystem.

Companion Planting: The practice of growing different plants together to benefit each other, such as pest control, pollination, and maximizing space.

Compost: Decomposed organic matter used to enrich soil and provide nutrients for plants.

Cover Crops: Plants grown primarily to improve soil health, manage soil erosion, and add organic matter to the soil.

Crop Rotation: The practice of growing different types of crops in the same area in sequential seasons to improve soil health and reduce pest and disease problems.

Dormancy: A period in a plant's life cycle when growth, development, and physical activity are temporarily stopped to conserve energy.

Ephemeris: A table or chart that shows the positions of celestial bodies at regular intervals, often used in astrology to plan gardening activities.

Foliar Feeding: The application of liquid fertilizer directly to plant leaves to provide nutrients quickly.

Germination: The process by which a seed develops into a new plant, beginning with the emergence of the seedling.

Green Manure: Cover crops that are grown to be plowed back into the soil to improve fertility and organic matter content.

Herbaceous Plants: Non-woody plants that die back to the ground each year and regrow from their root systems.

Hybrid: A plant produced by cross-pollinating two different plant varieties to create a new variety with desired traits.

Mulch: A layer of material, such as straw, leaves, or compost, spread over the soil surface to retain moisture, regulate soil temperature, and suppress weeds.

Organic Gardening: Gardening practices that avoid synthetic fertilizers and pesticides, focusing on natural methods to improve soil health and plant growth.

Perennials: Plants that live for more than two years, typically regrowing each season from the same root system.

Pollination: The transfer of pollen from the male parts of a flower to the female parts, resulting in fertilization and seed production.

Pruning: The practice of cutting back plant parts, such as branches or stems, to shape the plant, promote healthy growth, and remove dead or diseased material.

Raised Beds: Elevated garden beds that improve soil drainage, reduce compaction, and make gardening more accessible.

Soil Amendment: Materials added to soil to improve its physical or chemical properties, such as compost, lime, or gypsum.

Transplanting: Moving a plant from one location to another, typically from a seedling tray to the garden bed.

Astrological Terms

Air Signs: Gemini, Libra, and Aquarius. Associated with communication, intellect, and social interaction.

Ascendant (Rising Sign): The zodiac sign rising on the eastern horizon at the time of birth, influencing personality and outward behavior.

Astrological Chart: A diagram representing the positions of celestial bodies at a specific time and place, used in astrology to interpret influences on events and individuals.

Cardinal Signs: Aries, Cancer, Libra, and Capricorn. Associated with initiation, leadership, and action.

Celestial Events: Significant astronomical occurrences, such as eclipses, planetary alignments, and meteor showers, that influence astrological interpretations.

Conjunction: An aspect where two or more celestial bodies appear close together in the sky, amplifying their combined energy.

Cusp: The boundary between two zodiac signs or houses, representing a blend of influences from both.

Decan: A division of each zodiac sign into three ten-degree segments, adding nuance to astrological interpretations.

Earth Signs: Taurus, Virgo, and Capricorn. Associated with practicality, stability, and material concerns.

Eclipse: An astronomical event where one celestial body moves into the shadow of another, either blocking the sun (solar eclipse) or the moon (lunar eclipse).

Elements: The four fundamental qualities (fire, earth, air, water) that categorize the zodiac signs and influence their characteristics.

Ephemeris: A table or chart that shows the positions of celestial bodies at regular intervals, used to plan astrological gardening activities.

Fire Signs: Aries, Leo, and Sagittarius. Associated with energy, enthusiasm, and creativity.

Fixed Signs: Taurus, Leo, Scorpio, and Aquarius. Associated with stability, persistence, and determination.

Full Moon: The lunar phase when the moon is fully illuminated by the sun, symbolizing completion, abundance, and illumination.

House: One of the twelve divisions of the astrological chart, each representing different areas of life and influenced by the signs and planets within them.

Lunar Phases: The cyclic changes in the moon's appearance, including the New Moon, Waxing Crescent, First Quarter, Waxing Gibbous, Full Moon, Waning Gibbous, Last Quarter, and Waning Crescent.

Mutable Signs: Gemini, Virgo, Sagittarius, and Pisces. Associated with adaptability, flexibility, and change.

Natal Chart: An astrological chart created for the exact time and place of a person's birth, used to interpret individual characteristics and life path.

New Moon: The lunar phase when the moon is not visible from Earth, symbolizing new beginnings and potential.

Nodes (Lunar Nodes): The points where the moon's orbit intersects the ecliptic, associated with karmic lessons and life direction.

Opposition: An aspect where two celestial bodies are directly opposite each other in the sky, creating tension and the need for balance.

Planetary Hours: A system dividing the day and night into 24 hours, each ruled by a different planet, influencing specific activities.

Retrograde: The apparent backward motion of a planet in its orbit, often associated with delays, reflection, and revision.

Solar Return: The moment the sun returns to its exact position at the time of a person's birth, marking a new solar year and influencing the year ahead.

Solar Eclipse: An astronomical event where the moon passes between the Earth and the sun, blocking the sun's light and symbolizing transformation and change.

Solstice: The times of the year when the sun reaches its highest or lowest point in the sky at noon, marking the longest (Summer Solstice) and shortest (Winter Solstice) days.

Tropical Zodiac: The astrological system based on the Earth's seasons, dividing the ecliptic into twelve equal signs starting at the vernal equinox.

Trine: An aspect where two celestial bodies are 120 degrees apart, creating harmony and ease of expression.

Water Signs: Cancer, Scorpio, and Pisces. Associated with emotions, intuition, and sensitivity.

Waxing Moon: The lunar phase when the moon is increasing in illumination, symbolizing growth and development.

Waning Moon: The lunar phase when the moon is decreasing in illumination, symbolizing release and reflection.

Zodiac: The belt of the sky divided into twelve equal signs, each associated with specific characteristics and ruled by different planets.

Conclusion

This glossary provides definitions of key terms used throughout this book, covering both gardening and astrological concepts. Understanding these terms will help you integrate astrological principles into your gardening routine more effectively, allowing you to create a thriving, harmonious garden that aligns with the natural rhythms of the cosmos. As you continue your journey in astrological gardening, refer back to this glossary to deepen your understanding and enhance your practice.

Appendix B: Charts

This appendix provides useful charts for quick reference, including zodiac signs, planetary influences, moon phases, and celestial events. These charts will help you integrate astrological principles into your gardening routine effectively.

Zodiac Signs and Their Influences

Zodiac Sign	Element	Modality	Ruling Planet	Characteristics	Optimal Gardening Activities
Aries	Fire	Cardinal	Mars	Energetic, Initiating, Courageous	Planting fast-growing crops, starting new projects

Zodiac Sign	Element	Modality	Ruling Planet	Characteristics	Optimal Gardening Activities
Taurus	Earth	Fixed	Venus	Stable, Practical, Sensual	Planting root vegetables, enriching soil
Gemini	Air	Mutable	Mercury	Communicative, Adaptable, Curious	Planting climbing plants and herbs, companion planting

Zodiac Sign	Element	Modality	Ruling Planet	Characteristics	Optimal Gardening Activities
Cancer	Water	Cardinal	Moon	Nurturing, Intuitive, Protective	Planting leafy greens, watering and fertilizing
Leo	Fire	Fixed	Sun	Charismatic, Creative, Confident	Planting flowering plants, pruning and training

Zodiac Sign	Element	Modality	Ruling Planet	Characteristics	Optimal Gardening Activities
Virgo	Earth	Mutable	Mercury	Analytical, Health-conscious, Diligent	Planting medicinal herbs, soil testing and amending
Libra	Air	Cardinal	Venus	Harmonious, Diplomatic, Aesthetic	Planting ornamental flowers, balancing garden layout

Zodiac Sign	Element	Modality	Ruling Planet	Characteristics	Optimal Gardening Activities
Scorpio	Water	Fixed	Pluto	Intense, Transformative, Resourceful	Planting nightshades, composting and soil regeneration
Sagittarius	Fire	Mutable	Jupiter	Optimistic, Adventurous, Philosophical	Planting fruit trees, expanding garden areas

Zodiac Sign	Element	Modality	Ruling Planet	Characteristics	Optimal Gardening Activities
Capricorn	Earth	Cardinal	Saturn	Disciplined, Ambitious, Resilient	Planting trees, building garden structures
Aquarius	Air	Fixed	Uranus	Innovative, Humanitarian, Unconventional	Planting unusual or rare plants, experimenting with new techniques

Zodiac Sign	Element	Modality	Ruling Planet	Characteristics	Optimal Gardening Activities
Pisces	Water	Mutable	Neptune	Compassionate, Artistic, Intuitive	Planting aquatic plants, engaging in intuitive gardening

Planetary Influences on Gardening

Planet	Influence on Gardening	Best Practices
Sun	Vitality, Growth, Warmth	Planting, fertilizing, energy-intensive tasks

Planet	Influence on Gardening	Best Practices
Moon	Moisture, Emotion, Reflection	Watering, planting, harvesting, reflective practices
Mercury	Communication, Adaptability, Quick Growth	Planting herbs, fast-growing plants, companion planting
Venus	Beauty, Harmony, Aesthetics	Planting flowers, ornamental plants, soil enrichment
Mars	Energy, Action, Robustness	Planting hardy plants, pest control, pruning

Planet	Influence on Gardening	Best Practices
Jupiter	Expansion, Abundance, Growth	Planting fruit trees, expanding garden areas, fertilizing
Saturn	Discipline, Structure, Long-term Growth	Planting trees, building structures, soil regeneration
Uranus	Innovation, Change, Experimentation	Planting unusual plants, experimenting with new techniques
Neptune	Intuition, Sensitivity, Water	Planting aquatic plants, engaging in intuitive gardening

Planet	Influence on Gardening	Best Practices
Pluto	Transformation, Regeneration, Deep Fertility	Composting, soil regeneration, planting transformative crops

Moon Phases and Gardening Activities

Moon Phase	Symbolism	Optimal Gardening Activities
New Moon	New Beginnings	Planting seeds, starting new projects
Waxing Crescent	Growth and Expansion	Transplanting seedlings, nurturing young plants

Moon Phase	Symbolism	Optimal Gardening Activities
First Quarter	Strength and Stability	Pruning, training plants, strengthening growth
Waxing Gibbous	Preparation for Fullness	Enhancing soil health, ensuring plant vitality
Full Moon	Harvest and Abundance	Harvesting crops, significant garden projects, celebrating abundance
Waning Gibbous	Reflection and Rest	Completing harvesting, garden cleanup

Moon Phase	Symbolism	Optimal Gardening Activities
Last Quarter	Release and Reduction	Pruning, reducing dead plant material, preparing for new growth
Waning Crescent	Rest and Renewal	Resting, soil replenishment, planning for the next cycle

Celestial Events and Gardening

Celestial Event	Influence	Optimal Gardening Activities
Solar Eclipses	Transformation, Change	Reflecting on garden practices, planning new projects
Lunar Eclipses	Reflection, Release	Pruning, removing dead material, preparing for new growth
Planetary Alignments	Harmony, Growth	Enhancing soil health, planting new crops, balanced garden development

Celestial Event	Influence	Optimal Gardening Activities
Meteor Showers	Enrichment, Illumination	Enriching soil with cosmic dust, engaging in reflective practices

Combining Astrology and Gardening: Practical Examples
Example 1: Planting Tomatoes

- **Optimal Timing:** Plant tomato seeds during the New Moon in Cancer for moisture retention and growth.
- **Transplanting:** Transplant seedlings during the First Quarter in Leo for vigorous growth.
- **Fertilizing:** Apply organic fertilizers during the Waxing Gibbous in Virgo for strong root development.

Example 2: Harvesting Herbs

- **Optimal Timing:** Harvest herbs during the Full Moon for peak potency and flavor.
- **Preserving:** Begin drying and preserving herbs during the Waning Gibbous to extend their shelf life.

Example 3: Pruning Roses

- **Optimal Timing:** Prune roses during the First Quarter in Libra for balanced growth and structure.
- **Training:** Train climbing roses on trellises during the Waxing Crescent in Sagittarius for vigorous vertical growth.

Conclusion

These charts provide quick reference guides for integrating astrological principles into your gardening routine. By aligning your gardening activities with lunar phases, zodiac signs, planetary influences, and celestial events, you can enhance plant health, improve soil fertility, and create a harmonious and productive garden environment. Use these charts as a handy tool to guide your astrological gardening practices, helping you create a thriving garden that aligns with the natural rhythms of the cosmos.

Appendix C: Reading Material

This appendix provides a comprehensive list of recommended books, articles, and online resources for further reading on both astrology and gardening. These resources will help deepen your understanding of astrological principles and gardening practices, and guide you in integrating them into your gardening routine.

Recommended Books

Astrology

1. **"The Only Astrology Book You'll Ever Need" by Joanna Martine Woolfolk**
   - A comprehensive guide to astrology that covers everything from the basics to advanced concepts, including natal charts and planetary influences.
2. **"Parker's Astrology: The Definitive Guide to Using Astrology in Every Aspect of Your Life" by Julia and Derek Parker**
   - An in-depth resource on astrology that explores natal charts, planetary movements, and how astrology can be applied to various aspects of life.
3. **"Astrology for the Soul" by Jan Spiller**
   - Focuses on the role of the lunar nodes in astrology and how they influence personal growth and destiny.
4. **"The Twelve Houses: Exploring the Houses of the Horoscope" by Howard Sasportas**
   - A detailed exploration of the twelve houses in astrology and their significance in the natal chart.

5. **"Astrology, Psychology, and the Four Elements" by Stephen Arroyo**
   - Examines the connection between astrology, psychology, and the four elements (fire, earth, air, water), providing insights into personal development.

Gardening

1. **"The Vegetable Gardener's Bible" by Edward C. Smith**
   - A comprehensive guide to vegetable gardening that covers planning, planting, and maintaining a productive garden.
2. **"Carrots Love Tomatoes: Secrets of Companion Planting for Successful Gardening" by Louise Riotte**
   - Explores the benefits of companion planting and how different plants can benefit each other when grown together.
3. **"The Gardener's A-Z Guide to Growing Organic Food" by Tanya L.K. Denckla**
   - A detailed resource on organic gardening practices, including soil health, pest management, and crop rotation.
4. **"Biodynamic Gardening: For Health & Taste" by Hilary Wright**
   - An introduction to biodynamic gardening, combining organic gardening principles with astrological influences and holistic practices.
5. **"Gaia's Garden: A Guide to Home-Scale Permaculture" by Toby Hemenway**
   - Focuses on permaculture principles and how to create self-sustaining garden ecosystems.

Recommended Articles
Astrology

1. **"The Influence of the Moon on Agriculture" by Rudolf Steiner**
   - Explores the impact of lunar cycles on agriculture and how biodynamic principles can be applied to gardening.
2. **"Astrology and Gardening: The Lunar Connection" by Stephanie Gailing**
   - An article discussing the relationship between astrology and gardening, with practical tips on integrating lunar phases into gardening practices.
3. **"Zodiac Gardening: Planting by the Stars" by Jessica Walliser**
   - Provides an overview of how zodiac signs influence gardening activities and offers practical advice for aligning planting schedules with astrological cycles.

Gardening

1. **"The Science of Companion Planting" by Linda Gilkeson**
   - Examines the scientific basis of companion planting and its benefits for garden health and productivity.
2. **"The Benefits of Cover Crops" by Sustainable Agriculture Research and Education (SARE)**
   - Discusses the advantages of using cover crops to improve soil health, prevent erosion, and enhance biodiversity.
3. **"Organic Pest Control: The Basics" by Rodale Institute**
   - An introduction to organic pest control methods, including biological controls, natural pesticides, and integrated pest management.

Recommended Online Resources
Astrology

1. **Astro.com**
   - Offers free astrological charts, detailed horoscopes, and a wealth of articles on various astrological topics.
2. **Cafe Astrology**
   - Provides comprehensive astrological information, including birth charts, planetary transits, and compatibility reports.
3. **The Astrology Podcast**
   - A podcast featuring interviews with astrologers and discussions on a wide range of astrological topics.
4. **Astrology University**
   - Offers online courses, webinars, and workshops on astrology, taught by experienced astrologers.

Gardening

1. **Gardening Know How**
   - A comprehensive gardening resource with articles, guides, and tips on a wide range of gardening topics.
2. **Royal Horticultural Society (RHS)**
   - Provides expert advice on gardening, plant care, and horticultural practices, including a section on moon gardening.
3. **Mother Earth News**
   - Offers articles and resources on organic gardening, sustainable living, and homesteading.
4. **The Old Farmer's Almanac**
   - Includes gardening advice, planting calendars, and information on lunar phases and their influence on gardening.
5. **Permaculture Research Institute**

- Focuses on permaculture principles and practices, offering articles, courses, and resources on creating sustainable garden ecosystems.

Conclusion

This appendix provides a curated list of books, articles, and online resources to further your understanding of astrology and gardening. By exploring these resources, you can deepen your knowledge, refine your practices, and successfully integrate astrological principles into your gardening routine. Use these materials to continue your journey in astrological gardening, creating a thriving, harmonious garden that aligns with the natural rhythms of the cosmos.

<u>Message from the Author:</u>

I hope you enjoyed this book, I love astrology and knew there was not a book such as this out on the shelf. I love metaphysical items as well. Please check out my other books:

-Life of Government Benefits

-My life of Hell

-My life with Hydrocephalus

-Red Sky

-World Domination:Woman's rule

-World Domination:Woman's Rule 2: The War

-Life and Banishment of Apophis: book 1

-The Kidney Friendly Diet

-The Ultimate Hemp Cookbook

-Creating a Dispensary(legally)

-Cleanliness throughout life: the importance of showering from childhood to adulthood.

-Strong Roots: The Risks of Overcoddling children

-Hemp Horoscopes: Cosmic Insights and Earthly Healing

- Celestial Hemp Navigating the Zodiac: Through the Green Cosmos

-Astrological Hemp: Aligning The Stars with Earth's Ancient Herb

-The Astrological Guide to Hemp: Stars, Signs, and Sacred Leaves

-Green Growth: Innovative Marketing Strategies for your Hemp Products and Dispensary

-Cosmic Cannabis

-Astrological Munchies

-Henry The Hemp

-Zodiacal Roots: The Astrological Soul Of Hemp

- Green Constellations: Intersection of Hemp and Zodiac

-Hemp in The Houses: An astrological Adventure Through The Cannabis Galaxy

-Galactic Ganja Guide

Heavenly Hemp

Zodiac Leaves

Doctor Who Astrology

Cannastrology

Stellar Satvias and Cosmic Indicas

Celestial Cannabis: A Zodiac Journey

AstroHerbology: The Sky and The Soil: Volume 1

AstroHerbology:Celestial Cannabis:Volume 2

Cosmic Cannabis Cultivation

The Starry Guide to Herbal Harmony: Volume 1

The Starry Guide to Herbal Harmony: Cannabis Universe: Volume 2

Yugioh Astrology: Astrological Guide to Deck, Duels and more

Nightmare Mansion: Echoes of The Abyss

Nightmare Mansion 2: Legacy of Shadows

Nightmare Mansion 3: Shadows of the Forgotten

Nightmare Mansion 4: Echoes of the Damned

The Life and Banishment of Apophis: Book 2

Nightmare Mansion: Halls of Despair

Healing with Herb: Cannabis and Hydrocephalus

Planetary Pot: Aligning with Astrological Herbs: Volume 1

Fast Track to Freedom: 30 Days to Financial Independence Using AI, Assets, and Agile Hustles

Cosmic Hemp Pathways

How to Become Financially Free in 30 Days: 10,000 Paths to Prosperity

Zodiacal Herbage: Astrological Insights: Volume 1

Nightmare Mansion: Whispers in the Walls
The Daleks Invade Atlantis
Henry the hemp and Hydrocephalus

10X The Kidney Friendly Diet
Cannabis Universe: Adult coloring book
Hemp Astrology: The Healing Power of the Stars
Zodiacal Herbage: Astrological Insights: Cannabis Universe: Volume 2
<u>Planetary Pot: Aligning with Astrological Herbs: Cannabis Universes: Volume 2</u>
Doctor Who Meets the Replicators and SG-1: The Ultimate Battle for Survival
Nightmare Mansion: Curse of the Blood Moon
<u>The Celestial Stoner: A Guide to the Zodiac</u>
Cosmic Pleasures: Sex Toy Astrology for Every Sign
Hydrocephalus Astrology: Navigating the Stars and Healing Waters
Lapis and the Mischievous Chocolate Bar

Celestial Positions: Sexual Astrology for Every Sign
Apophis's Shadow Work Journal: **:** A Journey of Self-Discovery and Healing
Kinky Cosmos: Sexual Kink Astrology for Every Sign
Digital Cosmos: The Astrological Digimon Compendium

If you want solar for your home go here: https://www.harborso-lar.live/apophisenterprises/

Get Some Tarot cards: https://www.makeplayingcards.com/sell/apophis-occult-shop

Get some shirts: https://www.bonfire.com/store/apophis-shirt-emporium/

Instagrams:
@apophis_enterprises,
@hempkingdom2024,
@apophisbookemporium,
@apophisfashion,
@apophisscardshop

Twitter: @apophisenterpr1,

Tiktok:@apophisenterprise

Youtube: @sg1fan23477, @FiresideRetreatKingdom

Podcast: Apophis Chat Zone: https://open.spotify.com/show/5zXbrCLEV2xzCp8ybrfHsk?si=fb4d4fdbdce44dec

Newsletter: https://apophiss-newsletter-27c897.beehiiv.com/